# sponsor
# SUCCESS

## The WHATs and HOWs for business improvement projects

*A powerful & practical guide to delivering effective sponsorship of business improvement projects*

# DR MORGAN L JONES

A Cataloguing-in-Publication entry is available from the National Library of Australia.

Cover photo by iStock
Cover design and typeset by BookPOD
Printed and bound in Australia by BookPOD

ISBN: 978-0-9873477-0-1 (pbk)          eISBN: 978-0-9873527-1-2 (ebook)

*To Lizzie*

# Acknowledgements

I would like to acknowledge the following people: Janeece Keller for helping me in the early drafts and her honest feedback. To David Miller of Changefirst, thank you for your valuable feedback on sponsoring change; to George Lee Sye of Soarent Vision for encouraging me to write the book; to David Seacy of Interglobal Associates and Johnny Young for their challenging questions. I would also like to acknowledge the support and blunt feedback of Graeme Gherashe of the Octant Foundation.

Lastly I need to acknowledge the hundreds of Project Sponsors and senior managers that I have worked with over the years for sharing your challenges as Project Sponsors and for being open to my coaching. I have learnt so much. Also to the hundreds of Black and Green Belts that I have trained and coached for sharing their needs from Project Sponsors to facilitate effective delivery of their projects.

# Preface

## Why write this book?

I have been involved in the deployment of Six Sigma for over 10 years and have spent most of my working life driving change through organisations of various sizes. I was involved in the early deployment of Six Sigma at Caterpillar in the UK, before moving to rescue a failed deployment and then guide out-of-control deployments in New Zealand. Then I moved to a greenfield deployment in Australia as well as advising on a number of deployments in the South Pacific. These deployments were in construction, sales and marketing, transactional, government and logistics industries.

This book is the result of working with hundreds of managers in many organisations, who have been responsible for driving business improvement or change via individual projects and programs.

In my experience the most important factor in driving successful and sustainable change and business improvement through an organisation is the Sponsor. A Champion is the senior manager responsible for improvement within their part of the business. They typically oversee multiple initiatives simultaneously and own the resources and determine the approach and methodologies used to deliver the projects. In some organisations this role is called a Sponsor in others Champion, for simplicity I will use the name Sponsor throughout this book as this is focused on the manager responsible for the change.

Most projects that run through Six Sigma, Lean or Business Transformation programs have a single senior manager responsible for the improvement program as well as a project manager (who may be Six Sigma Black Belt trained) to deliver individual projects. Failure to assign a skilled individual to sponsor a Six Sigma initiative most certainly spells project failure.

Most business improvement initiatives and projects fail when the Sponsor delegates the project, then walks away expecting the project manager or Black Belt to deliver the project unsupported. Through my research and experience, I've found that when the Sponsor maintains project ownership throughout its duration, only then a project becomes successful. It takes a great deal of training, experience and preparation to become an effective Sponsor.

## Why this is important

"Doing more with less, better" is a typical objective of business executives or owners pursuing a continuous improvement strategy. Forward-thinking companies have invested in implementing Lean Six Sigma as a competitive and strategic opportunity to transform their businesses amid the recession. These companies see Lean Six Sigma as the key to reducing waste, improving cash flow and improving operational flexibility, thus enabling them to adjust more quickly to the new realities of today's economic climate.

I like to compare an organisation to the human body. Both are complex entities made up of many parts that need to work in harmony to grow and develop. Achieving peak performance requires a body to be healthy and good health is made up of three key areas: physical, mental and spiritual health. How this can align organisationally is:

- Physical health – Processes that deliver service/product

- Mental health – Policies, procedures and plan (methodology)

- Spiritual health – Organisational culture

In order to maintain a healthy body, one must ensure a balanced and aligned interaction of these interdependent components. One must also focus on changing habits from the inside out and not the other way around. For example, one undergoes more than merely superficial changes (e.g. liposuction) to lose weight. Radical changes such as addressing spiritual and mental health problems are also needed to fix the root cause of weight issues. Liposuction will fix the symptom of physical appearance but unless attitudes and behaviour change, then the old lifestyle that generated this symptom will put weight back on again. So the key is to change the internal thinking process that changes behaviours to improve eating habits and physical exercise.

Good physical health could be achieved by going to the gym, cutting out the biscuits, generally eating healthier and getting the right amount of sleep. This is analogous to business processes having appropriate resources, good training and processes to add value to products or services that customers require from the organisation.

Mental health on a personal level is all about maintaining the intellectual capacity to assist the body to function effectively in our environments. Similarly in organisations, this equates to having the proper policies, procedures and plans in place to keep the processes functioning correctly.

Finally, there is spiritual health which is very often ignored both in a personal and organisational context. Personally, poor spiritual health results in individuals behaving or acting in a way that is not aligned with their values and beliefs. Increasingly, this is often associated with unhealthy levels of stress. The way this plays out in organisations is identical to the individual situation where there is an incongruity between what is said and what is done.

This analogy will help us understand the critical role the Sponsor has on the journey to a healthy organisation. And as the journey is permeated by different degrees and levels of change, the Sponsor's role as a change agent becomes more and more crucial. He or she has to have an arsenal of skills and strategies, the WHATs and the HOWs, to combat obstacles to organisational health and the enemies of organisational change.

*Chapter 1* of this book gives a bird's eye view of the multiple roles of a Sponsor and situates his or her functions in the realm of Lean Six Sigma. *Chapter 2* describes the Lean Six Sigma process and elaborates on the specific responsibilities of the Sponsor throughout the DMAIC process (Define – Measure – Analyse – Improve – Control). Arguing that Lean Six Sigma is both the product and cause of change, *Chapter 3* offers a framework for understanding the dynamics of organisational change and the rudiments of change management. Conceding that wearing the hat of a change agent is the most challenging role of the Sponsor, two sections are devoted to explaining the skills and strategies that the Sponsor must use in sponsoring change. *Chapter 4* presents the four critical skills needed (WHATs) and *Chapter 5* proposes four useful strategies (HOWs). The 4 WHATs include tenets that the Sponsor must uphold: Clarity, Criticality, Commitment and Consistency. The 4 HOWs are specific tools and techniques that the Sponsor must employ: Charter, Change, Coaching and Communication. *Chapter 6* explores how these 8 Cs can be most effectively applied in problematic situations. *Chapter 7* provides a discussion on how to improve one's sponsoring skills. In conclusion, *Chapter 8* underscores the most significant points that resonate throughout this book, most specifically those factors that lead to Sponsor success. Some practical tools and guidelines are appended for easy reference.

I have highlighted some points through personal anecdotes, professional "war stories" and analogies. I liken a Project Sponsor to a Celebrity Chef who has his or her name associated with their restaurant. Though they don't do all the cooking or may not even be there physically, their reputation is always on the line. Even when they have delegated the day-to-day cooking to a local lead chef, a good Sponsor's reputation is as much on the line as the Celebrity Chef's. One bad project, like a bad meal, can really damage the reputation of the Sponsor.

## Who should read this book?

Anyone with a desire to improve the health of their organisation, department or team should read this book. More specifically, the principles, approach, methodology, thoughts and tools are a valuable resource for three groups of people within any organisation:

- Executives wanting to get more out of their business improvement projects.

- Senior managers who are looking to create a more responsive/agile business in response to changing customer requirements and expectations.

- Team leaders or managers responsible for delivering sustainable improvements and savings (human element).

- Green and Black Belts wanting to get the best support from their Sponsors.

- Master Black Belts wanting to develop the skills and effectiveness of their Sponsors.

- Anyone who believes they want to improve their Sponsor skills.

- Anyone new to sponsoring business improvement projects.

## Who will benefit from reading this book?

Anyone with an interest in deploying Lean Six Sigma within their organisation will get value from reading this book. In particular it has been written for:

- Any business, irrespective of size or industry group, that values customers, people, time and resources.

- Businesses that are frustrated with their sluggish performance, long lead times, high inventory levels and silo cultures.

- Organisations that have tried business improvement initiatives and fallen short or failed.

- Organisations looking for sustainability in business improvement rather than the regular cost cutting exercises.

# Contents

# 1

# Introduction

Six Sigma is an integrated, disciplined and proven approach to business improvement. It provides roadmaps, methods, tools and techniques to optimise organisational effectiveness and efficiency given the organisation's current resources.

Globalisation and systematic changes in international trade infrastructure, coupled with unprecedented scientific and technological advances in many fields, have intensified market competition on a global scale. The imperatives of global competitiveness continue to increase pressure on organisations not just to supersede their rivals, but merely to survive. As such, a worker's job requires not only getting their day-to-day activities done, but also improving how they do it. One of the most effective methods of improving organisational performance is Six Sigma.

Six Sigma is a management methodology and data driven approach that aims to deliver high levels of customer satisfaction. It is centred on a portfolio of projects that produce measurable business results and improve organisational processes by understanding, predicting and controlling variation. The ultimate aim of Six Sigma is to improve product and service quality to differentiate the organisation over the long term.

Six Sigma requires processes and performance to be measured differently to any traditional performance metrics, shifting the focus from outputs and budgets to process capability, product design and overall quality.

A holistic approach to business improvement, Six Sigma requires a "systems perspective" for driving change. All interactive functions, units and processes within the business need to be viewed together and aligned to work in synergy.

There are both financial and non-financial benefits of successful Six Sigma programs. The benefits are achieved because, at its core, Six Sigma is about:

- Designing (or redesigning) a business so the customer is at the centre of all activities.
- Putting rigour and structure into the delivery of discrete pieces of work.
- Fact-based decision-making and holding people accountable to what they've said they would do.
- Building the capability of the people for the future.
- Ensuring all the key activities align to the business strategy so you can prioritise what's important rather than just doing pet projects.
- Any benefits that are achieved are sustainable over the longer term.

For a Six Sigma project to succeed, it needs to employ the services of a **Sponsor** and the support of a **Champion**, although depending on the scope of a project, the roles of the Sponsor and Champion could be rolled into one person. The Champion is the project advocate who "sponsors" the project while the Sponsor who has a substantial stake in the project outcome "owns" the project. The Project Sponsor is usually a senior leader or one who heads a certain functional area thus has formal authority and ownership of the process sought to be improved.

Sponsors are chiefly responsible for deployment of Six Sigma within organisations. They identify, propose and assess potential projects that are aligned with the goals of the organisation, set priorities, and lead project planning, strategising and implementation to maximise benefits and ensure project success.

In today's business world, what is expected of a Sponsor role has shied away from them being an expert with access to vast amounts of knowledge and data. The Sponsor's role is now to create three new things for the project: business context, business or department relevance and individual meaning, and then to help the team to capture this succinctly and package and deliver this in a way that is truly understood. Anyone can come up with a great improvement idea, usually Sponsors and Champions but others can also come up with the same ideas. It is the person who turns that idea into something beneficial to the organisation that makes the difference.

For large-scale projects, there may be several Champions but only one Sponsor. In several instances, however, there may only be one person performing the roles of both Sponsor and Champion. Again, for brevity and simplicity, the word Sponsor is used throughout this book.

## The Responsibility of the Six Sigma Sponsor

The Project Sponsor is usually a senior level manager trained in the essentials of Six Sigma. Their role is to promote and lead the deployment of Six Sigma in an area of the business. For organisation wide Six Sigma initiatives to succeed, they must involve all units and levels of the business.

Six Sigma projects are facilitated by teams whose members are trained to provide fact-based decision-making information to the business. A Six Sigma project team usually includes representatives from the leadership teams of the impacted business units, Black Belts, Green Belts, and a Sponsor. How the members of the project team interact and work together needs to be clearly defined. *Figure 1.1* illustrates the interactive relationships of the key roles in a Six Sigma project.

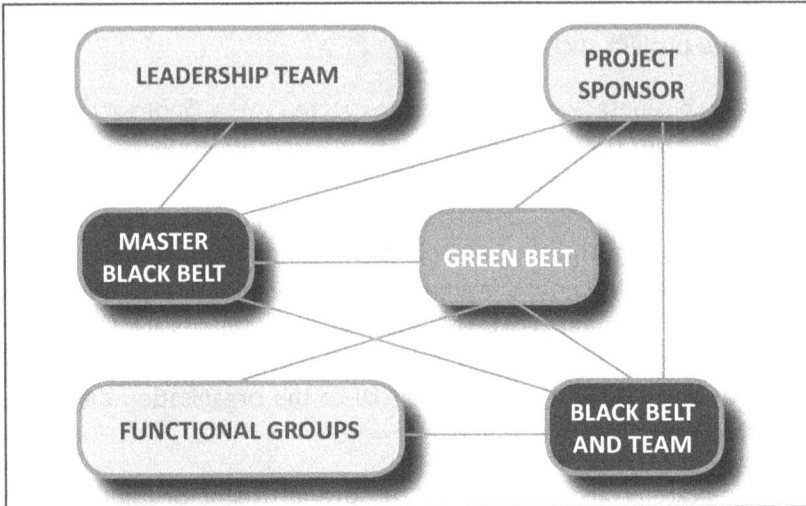

*Figure 1.1 – The Interrelationships of the Members of a Six Sigma Team*

The leadership team (sometimes called the Six Sigma Council or steering panel) leads the overall effort and has responsibility for approving the projects undertaken by Black Belts. In the case of a project based primarily in the finance division, the leadership team might be the Chief Financial Officer and selected members of the finance department.

The Master Black Belt is a Six Sigma expert responsible for Six Sigma strategy, training, mentoring, deployment and results. The Master Black Belt may be full-time, part-time or a contractor.

A Black Belt is a fully trained Six Sigma expert who performs much of the technical analysis required of the Six Sigma project and may be full-time or part-time in the role. The Green Belt is a functional employee trained in introductory Six Sigma tools and methodology and works on projects part-time.

Six Sigma functional groups refer to the individuals from various functional units (e.g. supply chain, finance, human resources etc.) who support specific projects. It is important that team members are selected from all functional areas affected by the Six Sigma project.

Since a Six Sigma project has cross-functional impact, the Sponsor must have charisma and political influence as well as sufficient authority to effectively inspire enthusiasm to change and to allocate organisational resources. The project's outcome is largely determined by the Project Sponsor.

The Sponsor should be named right at the start of the Lean Six Sigma project because organisational resistance may start even before the project. Cynicism, resentment and negativity already in people's minds can destabilise the project right from the outset if the Sponsor isn't on board to manage expectations and communications.

The Project Sponsor is the unifying force that keeps the project team on track during the course of the project and balances the needs of the project with the day-to-day running of the business. Maintaining team focus and steering the project to success means the Project Sponsor needs to assume multiple roles.

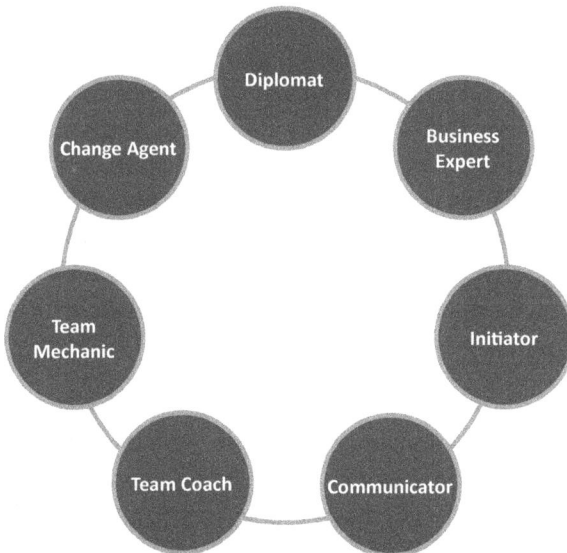

*Figure 1.2 – Multiple Roles of a Project Sponsor*

As a diplomat, the Project Sponsor serves as the team negotiator. He or she is the *unblocker* who clears the way for smooth implementation of changes by removing roadblocks and neutralising or minimising resistance. He or she is the *mediator* who must resolve conflicts among people affected by the change and serves as a conduit between project team and senior management. He or she is also the conduit between the project team and management and all other organisational units, ensuring that the project team is not isolated from the rest of the business and that the Six Sigma initiative is clearly understood by all stakeholders. To do this, the Sponsor must mediate any issues between the Black Belts and top management as well as conflict within the project team. The Project Sponsor's role allows the Black Belts and the Green Belts to concentrate on their areas of the project and on developing creative solutions. Sponsors are typically in a position to convince senior management of the relevance of an initiative to organisational goals and explain the viability of proposed Six Sigma projects.

To be an effective project implementer, the Project Sponsor must be a business expert who must plan and execute the smooth deployment of the Lean Six Sigma initiative and integrate the project into the organisation. Acting as project owner, they sign off and allocate the resources needed to implement the project. With this authority comes the responsibility to observe and be able to identify difficulties and weaknesses at the early stages of project planning. Part of the Sponsor's role in project implementation is to assess the project status from an executive viewpoint, tracking timelines, budget tolerances, resource availability, and benchmarks. The Project Sponsor ensures that the project proceeds as planned, augments resources as needed, and initiates redirections when necessary.

The Project Sponsor is the chief communicator. The Sponsor removes barriers to communication and encourages critical thinking and feedback to thrash out problems and avoid conflicting ideas and decisions. With respect to initiating change, the Sponsor acts as a *visionary*. The Sponsor presents his vision of the new future, sells how this new future could be achieved, and inspires people to share the Sponsor's vision and work with him or her to reach this vision.

As a team coach, the Project Sponsor determines required skills, finds resources, and hones specific competencies to sustain commitment and allow team members to meet performance standards and project benchmarks. The repertoire of a coaching Sponsor consists of leadership competence and outstanding interpersonal skills. Coaching through organisational change, the Sponsor must actively participate in planning the change, as well as the strategies on how to implement the change successfully.

As a team mechanic, the Project Sponsor ensures that the members of the team work like a well-oiled machine that has the endurance to withstand significant pressures over the duration of the project. Thus, the Sponsor is a team builder who solicits cooperative participation to keep the team spirit alive.

Perhaps one of the most crucial functions of a Project Sponsor is managing change. As a change agent, the Project Sponsor ensures that the members of the organisation understand and accept the changes that the Six Sigma project requires. The Project Sponsor leads change and shows commitment to adapt to any change in order to motivate people to follow his lead. The Sponsor models the adaptive behaviour and should "walk the walk". To be an effective change manager, the Sponsor needs to understand the members of the project team, contextualise the major change into impacts for each individual, identify motivational factors and forms of resistance, and steer the organisation to embrace the change and leverage its benefits. The Sponsor is the leader who should serve as a role model for the members of the organisation and be actively involved in all stages of the change.

A chef heads the culinary staff and wears different hats (as well as an apron) not only to maximise the potentials of the workers in the kitchen but also to enhance the services of the whole dining establishment. Similarly, the Sponsor dons a variety of hats in overseeing a Six Sigma project from initiation to completion and does have to deal not only with the work team but also with the whole organisation and even with external factors and elements. The most vital hat would be the one that allows the Sponsor to manage change successfully.

Steering a Lean Six Sigma project to success is a complicated task. The Sponsor has to deal with all the stress, risks and stakes that the accompanying change entails. Change dawns right at the start of the project and will continue to impact through the project life cycle. In fact, change could very well be the impetus of a Lean Six Sigma project and its only certain and inevitable result. Managing change becomes a core competence of sponsoring. Therefore, an astute understanding of not only the rudiments of Six Sigma and Lean business improvement processes but also of the dynamics of change management will help the Sponsor negotiate the risks and challenges of project deployment, reinforce changes, and amplify long-term success. The next chapter discusses the Lean Six Sigma process, and is followed by the chapter on change management concepts.

# 2

## Getting Faster and Cheaper to Get Better Through Lean Six Sigma

Before embarking on your Lean journey as a Sponsor, it is necessary to understand the Lean Six Sigma process. Lean Six Sigma raises the Six Sigma process to a higher notch by not only harnessing quality but also speed. I would say that Lean Six Sigma is the marriage of Lean and Six Sigma, the union of speed and quality. Another way of describing it is that Lean Six Sigma results in quality products and services with minimal or no defects in the fastest possible time. To incorporate Lean Six Sigma, a company may start off with integrating Six Sigma in business improvement and then follows on with Lean manufacturing or Lean transformation in specific project cycles or program components. Or, it will first apply Lean concepts to identify and remove waste and increase process velocity, then use Six Sigma rigour to identify and remove process variation.

As a combined approach, Lean Six Sigma pursues the synergy of Six Sigma techniques that focus on quality and Lean tools that focus on increasing process efficiency to optimise the improvement process. By using both approaches, organisations amplify the strengths and rectify the flaws of the individual techniques of each methodology.

Lean Six Sigma aggressively pursues value added processes and eliminates non-value added processes (those that cause delay, waste and poor quality, for example). Lean Six Sigma may be used by business organisations, whether in the manufacturing, services or transactional industries. For example, businesses may aim to reduce manufacturing costs from 20 to 50 percent, improve response time by 50 percent, accelerate service delivery by 30 percent, or expand production capacity by 30 percent without procuring more machinery or hiring more workers, perhaps simply by cleaning up work space. Put simply, Lean Six Sigma allows the organisation to produce goods and services of utmost quality through a process map in the shortest amount of time possible.

The incremental process improvement used in Lean Six Sigma is the DMAIC Method. DMAIC is an acronym that stands for Define – Measure – Analyse – Improve – Control. The Project Sponsor should have a good grasp of the elements of each stage in the DMAIC process.

## The DMAIC Roadmap

The key concept in the DMAIC Model is process, and its key tenet is process improvement to meet performance standards and satisfy customer requirements. Process is its main focus because all organisational activities can be analysed and understood as a process or series of processes. The DMAIC roadmap identifies and improves those processes that are strategically important – those processes that add value to goods and services and meet customer expectations.

The problem needing to be solved must be specifically defined and expressed in quantitative terms so that on completion, the improvements can be measured. For projects that aim to improve processes, Lean Six Sigma project teams follow the DMAIC Model as their roadmap to determine the root cause of a problem and then they apply various tools and techniques to find a solution.

By using the DMAIC method to solve problems, companies come to understand chronic problems or performance gaps that exist in a process. Following the roadmap means that the key upstream variables (referred to as Xs) in a process are identified and the ones that most significantly impact the outcome (referred to as critical to quality or CTQs or output metrics Ys) are improved. Project managers optimise the relationships between the CTQ Xs and the outcomes to improve the process and customer experience.

The methodology requires that at each stage of the project, the project team presents their findings to the Project Sponsor and any relevant steering committee before proceeding to the next phase. The key purposes of each stage are provided in *Table 2.1*.

| STEPS | PURPOSES |
|---|---|
| **DEFINE** | ▪ Define the problem, the process and the project outcomes<br>▪ Identify what's important, determine what's going wrong and how it is affecting the customer |
| **MEASURE** | ▪ Collect data on the current performance<br>▪ Identify what the current situation is |
| **ANALYSE** | ▪ Analyse data to determine cause and effect<br>▪ Analyse what is really going wrong, i.e. root cause rather than symptom |
| **IMPROVE** | ▪ Improve by taking action<br>▪ Fix what's going wrong and demonstrate via a pilot |
| **CONTROL** | ▪ Control process implementation to guarantee performance and sustainability<br>▪ Verify gains and process improvements |

*Table 2.1 – The DMAIC Step-by-Step Process*

## Tollgate Reviews

Lean Six Sigma projects should be evaluated regularly and reviews should be done after each step in the improvement process. Tollgate reviews are milestones that have clearly specified objectives, and on successful completion of them the project is allowed to pass through the gate or to the next stage of the improvement process. If the objectives aren't met, the project should remain at a particular phase until all criteria and deliverables have been satisfied. Installing checkpoints enhances the clarity and criticality of the entire project. Milestone checklists for each phase are given in *Appendix 1*.

As the gatekeeper, the Project Sponsor is tasked to review the progress of the team and to tackle questions at each phase of the DMAIC cycle. A well-structured questioning strategy will make the most out of each opportunity.

Key benefits of conducting tollgate reviews are shown in *Table 2.2*.

| | |
|---|---|
| *Continuous Monitoring* | *A project review allows continuous monitoring of the team's progress and serves as a continuous reminder of where the group is and what still needs to be done. Project monitoring brings focus and synergy to group effort. Failure to monitor progress prevents the team from addressing mistakes and problems immediately.* |
| *Guidance and Direction* | *A project review is both a guidance tool and insurance tool that will guide the group members in performing their duties and that will ensure that the team is moving in the right direction.* |
| *Alignment of Activities* | *A project review provides real time collaboration and communication. Each phase in the DMAIC cycle is composed of a series of activities, separate functions and responsibilities, and different working sub-groups and team leaders, therefore there is a need to align the array of activities towards the common objective.* |
| *Clearing the Way* | *A project review allows the Sponsor to remove roadblocks and to resolve conflicts and issues that impede progress and completion. Particular emphasis is placed on those problems resulting in resistance to change.* |
| *Sharing Best Practice* | *A project review allows the team members to learn from each other and perhaps from subject matter experts. The organisation also can share best practice from the project team.* |
| *Motivation and Support* | *A project review allows the Sponsor to recognise and reward as job well done and motivate the members to keep progressing the project.* |
| *Integrity of Decisions* | *A project review ensures that evidence is presented to support decisions. Decisions should not be made in a vacuum in the absence of facts and data.* |

*Table 2.2 – Benefits of Tollgate Reviews*

Who should attend the review?

It is important that a project review is attended by all those who are involved in the process so that all perspectives will be understood and that all concerned people, especially the key decision-makers, are well-informed and updated. The list of attendees should include the following:

- Project leader (Green or Black Belt)
- Project Sponsor
- Master Black Belt
- Selected members of management

What to expect from the project team

The success of the review also depends on the team's preparation. Prior to the presentation, the team should prepare the following and have them ready:

- Venue
- Presentation equipment
- Storyboard presentation (already practised)
- Supporting documents, data, information
- Summary of results of previous tollgate reviews/meetings

How will the meeting proceed?

The project manager should send out the agenda and meeting invites and the following format is suggested for the structure of the proceedings:

> **GUIDELINES FOR SUCCESSFUL TOLLGATE REVIEWS**
>
> *Clarity of purpose*
> *Focus on critical issues and deliverables*
> *Collegiality (not hostile investigation)*
> *Honest discussion*
> *Constructive criticism*
> *Good listening skills*
> *Data-driven presentation and discussion*

1. Introduction by Project Sponsor
- Setting the stage for the review, as well as highlighting the importance of the project

2. Project Team Presentation
- Summary of previous reviews
- Review of the current phase
- In informal meetings, questions/points of clarification may be asked intermittently or in between topics (if it is a formal meeting, the reviewers wait until the team finishes with their presentation)

3. Reviewer Comments (if formal presentation)
- Identification of accomplishments and positive points
- Clarification questions
- Identification of weaknesses, flaws, loopholes, deficiencies, and/or failures
- Recommendations for improvement or completion
- Sign-off of the phase if warranted; if not, the sign-off is deferred until such time that requirements are met or recommendations are complied with

4. Closing by Project Sponsor
- Reminders
- Words of support and encouragement

## The Art of Questioning

Asking good questions is a key management skill. Poor questions therefore translate to poor management. Although success is a result of several factors, skill in questioning would certainly boost the Sponsor's chance for success. To be an effective coach, the Project Sponsor, equipped with their senior management experience, can assist the project team to discover more innovative and effective ways to solve problems and address business challenges.

**Ten Basic Rules for Asking Questions:**

1.  Be direct.

2.  Make eye contact if asking the question in person.

3.  Use plain language.

4.  Use simple sentence structure.

5.  Be brief.

6.  Maintain focus on the subject at hand.

7.  Make certain the purpose of the question is clear.

8.  Make certain the question is appropriate for the person and for the situation.

9.  Ensure the manner of asking reflects the intent.

10. Know what to do with the answer.


If there is any doubt about the question being asked or if the Sponsor feels that their question isn't being answered, they should either:

-  Repeat the question,
-  Rephrase the question, or
-  Restructure the question.

Questioning allows the business to find out what it needs to know. The simple formula is – good questions plus good answers equals success. Examples of questions that could be asked by the Sponsor at each tollgate review are provided in the succeeding discussions.

## The DEFINE Phase

This is the initial stage of the DMAIC process where the Lean Six Sigma team clarifies the purpose and scope of the project. The team defines the problem area, estimates resources needed to complete the project, identifies the people that need to be involved, and establishes a timeline. It is also during "DEFINE" that a project team is trained in Six Sigma and Lean and becomes committed to the change initiative and supported by the management. Or, in cases where the team has had previous Lean Six Sigma experience, a short review should be conducted to stress effective methodologies, tools and techniques that drive results and sustainability.

Key Roles of the Sponsor in **DEFINE**

Visionary
Unblocker
Planner
Business Expert
Communicator
Change Agent

Resistance to, lack of knowledge of, and doubts about the need for the Lean Six Sigma initiative are best settled at the start of the Define Phase. This is done through training and the support of an experienced Six Sigma coach, e.g. Black or Master Black Belt. The Sponsor's role at this stage is to create a mindshare rather than to simply impose, although passivity should never be an option. Team members with previous experience in Lean Six Sigma may take offence when they are being taught what they already know. The Sponsor instead has to show a supportive stance and help situate the team members in the correct support environment.

The type and degree of support a project team needs during the Define Phase will depend on the skill and knowledge level of the members, the experiential level of the organisation in Lean Six Sigma, the resources available at their disposal, and the nature and complexity of the task at hand, among others. The Sponsor gives support to the project team by ensuring that division of work is done fairly and equitably and that the members are assigned to tasks they are most capable or qualified in. In instances where knowledge and skills are lacking, the Sponsor has to push for Lean Six Sigma education and training as needed.

The steps, tools and outputs of the Define Phase are summarised in *Table 2.3*. Tools and techniques in each step of the DMAIC process will not be discussed in great detail but most are defined in the glossary for ready reference. The Sponsor guides the team in selecting the right tools and techniques to be used.

| Key Steps in the Define Phase | Tools/Techniques the Project Team May Use | Typical Project Team Deliverables |
|---|---|---|
| Define problem statement and evolve problem fact sheet, goals and final benefits | • VOC<br>• Stakeholder Analysis<br>• SIPOC Diagram | Defined problem |
| Define customers and identify CTQs | • Pareto<br>• CTQ Flow down<br>• CTQ Definitions | Project CTQs |
| Work out a project plan and develop project charter | • Project Charter<br>• DMAIC Work Breakdown | Approved team charter |
| Develop and document a detailed "as is" process map | Structure<br>• Process Flowchart/<br>Spaghetti Diagram<br>• Profit by Product<br>• Defect Rate<br>• SPC Data | High level process map |

*Table 2.3 – Steps, Tools and Deliverables in Process Definition*

One of the most important purposes of the Define Phase is the identification of CTQs (critical to quality outputs). In Lean Six Sigma projects, a CTQ is interpreted from a qualitative customer statement to be an actionable, quantitative business specification. Failure of a product or service to conform to a CTQ indicates a defect and leads to customer dissatisfaction.

Problem areas in a business are typically gleaned from customer complaints, and from data on reject rates, waste, inventory, downtime, process costs etc. In identifying the problem area and project CTQs, the team first determines who the customers of the process in question are and their requirements. The problem definition will become clearer once process mapping is done and the material and data flow has been studied.

The project charter is a very important document that may only be one page but is used to succinctly sell the project objective so that all involved have the same understanding.

The project charter consists of the following:

- Business case or value proposition
- Problem statement
- Goal statement
- Scope
- Milestones and schedule
- Benefits
- Roles and responsibilities
- Project objective

The project charter should be clear on specific roles and responsibilities of the project team members to avoid misunderstanding and to ensure accountability, and should also describe role expectations of other organisational units. It also details protocols, communication channels and decision-making mechanisms. The project charter should be based on a careful estimation of strategic impact without which the focus, direction and legitimacy of the project are at risk.

## What does a Sponsor need to see to pass a project through the Define Phase?

The following set of questions should allow the sponsor to get some real clarity and be able to make the decision whether to allow the project to progress to the next phase. It is recommended that the questions are asked in the order presented here, however it is also important to ensure the presentation flows.

### Deliverable: Problem statement

- What problem or gap are you addressing?
- Why is the project important?
- Have constraints and key assumptions been identified?
- What are the business reasons for completing the project?

### Deliverable: Project scope

- What is in scope?
- What is out of scope?
- Is this achievable in the timeframe?
- Who are the stakeholders and how will they be involved in the project? Have they expressed agreement and support to the project?

### Deliverable: Project CTQs

- Who are the customers?
- What data do you have to understand customer requirements?
- Have the customer needs been translated into specific, measurable requirements? How?
- What impact will closing the gap or solving the problem have on customers?

### Deliverable: Measures of success

- How will success be measured?
- How will we know that we have met customer requirements?
- At the end of the Improve Phase, what are we going to see that's different?
- What will I get in my hand as proof of the change?

### Team Readiness

In addition to the above project deliverables, it is at the onset of the Define Phase that the Project Sponsor should evaluate the readiness of the team members to conduct the Lean Six Sigma project. The following questions could be used as a guide when reviewing team readiness:

- Who are the team members? Have they expressed commitment to the project and has this committed support been conveyed to the Project Sponsor?
- Is the team adequately staffed with the desired cross-functionality? If not, what additional resources are available to the team?
- Does the team know how to address constraints and perceived difficulties during the course of the project?

- How does the team track and document its work?

Completing the Define Phase successfully is the first big step to project success. Defining the right thing to do and how to do it the right way is the first step to paving the way to ultimate success. The Sponsor should ensure that at the end of the Define Phase, project purpose and scope have been set, processes that need to be changed and opportunities for business improvement have been identified, schedules, functions and accountabilities have been established, and more importantly, the project team, including the Sponsor, is convinced of the vision and the likelihood of success. In this stage, the Sponsor acts as a visionary, unblocker, planner, business expert, communicator and change agent. He or she must attempt to address all possible constraints at this stage.

## The MEASURE Phase

Bad data leads to bad decisions, bad decisions lead to bad project outcomes and bad project outcomes lead to bad business results.

Six Sigma is all about data-driven decision-making and the success of a Six Sigma initiative relies greatly on the adequacy and reliability of data. Failure by a project team to gather sufficient reliable data on the current state of the process (or the size of the problem) spells catastrophe because the team starts on the wrong foot. Projects can fail if bad or incorrect data is collected because it prevents the project team from identifying the true root cause and that means that improvements that won't have a lasting impact may be implemented – wasting time, money and effort for all involved. Multiple data sources are a must during Measure Phase. Take this example: In a chemical company which was facing a number of lawsuits due to contaminated products a project team was assigned to study how different qualities of a product were affected by factors in any

Key Roles of the Sponsor in **MEASURE**

Business Expert
Coach
Planner
Initiator
Communicator

stage of the chemical processing. Initial analysis showed that temperature in different stages of the process may affect particular characteristics of a chemical substance. However, further investigations showed that the problem arose from the contaminated delivery trucks they had outsourced. Imagine if the team only focused on internal processes.

During the Measure Phase the team assesses current process performance and quantifies the problem so that the factors that most influence the outcome are identified. It is in this stage that the project team gathers and analyses as much information as possible on the current process to understand how it works and how well it works, in other words, the current performance standards. Typically, the team starts the Measure Phase with process mapping or drawing a process flowchart to enable them to appreciate the components, inputs, throughputs, outputs, and controls of the process. The steps typically performed in the Measure Phase are summarised in *Table 2.4*.

| Key Steps in the Measure Phase | Tools/Techniques the Project Team May Use | Typical Project Team Deliverables |
|---|---|---|
| Identify CTQ characteristic | • Fishbone, FMEA, Pareto Customer, QFD | Project Y |
| Define performance standards | • Customer<br>• Blueprints<br>• Process Flowchart<br>• Benchmarking<br>• Process Sigma Calculation | Performance standard for Project Y |
| Establish data collection plan, validate measurement system and collect data | • MSA<br>• Gage Study<br>Lean tools: Value Stream Mapping, Value Stream Costing, Value-Added to Non-Value-Added Ratio, CT/VT, CT/TAKT Time, Current Reality Trees, Inventory Turnover Rate, Total Productive Maintenance | Data collection plan and MSA |

*Table 2.4 – Steps, Tools and Deliverables in Process Measurement*

The Measure Phase often includes analysis of well understood Xs and as such the team will develop an initial explanation of the relationships of some of the variables on the project outcome. The relationship is often referred to as $Y=f(X)$ where Y represents the outputs (Y) and the inputs (Xs) and their relationship on the output Xs.

To make sure the measurement system being used to define the problem is understood, the project team needs to carry out Measurement Systems Analysis (MSA).

Resistance to data collection typically arises during the Measure Phase when team members get overwhelmed with the volume of data (and sometimes unavailability of data) being measured and analysed, or when they are not convinced they will find a solution to the problem, or when they don't completely understand the current process. As a result, the members may resort to short cuts and easier routes resulting in skewed or inaccurate data and invalid results. Sometimes, resistance could also arise from the side of management. It is the Project Sponsor's role to put the members back on track through coaching, clarifying guidelines and rule setting, brainstorming and rigorous monitoring, and to coordinate with management through straightforward discussions. The Project Sponsor should ensure that both team members and management agree on how the process is currently performing and that it is able to be improved. These data should be used to revisit the problem statement and project charter and make modifications as may be necessary.

## What a Sponsor should expect from a Measure Project Review

The Measure Phase is all about understanding how capable a process is of currently meeting the customer's needs. The following set of questions should allow the Sponsor to get some real clarity and be able to make a decision to allow the project to progress to the next phase. It is recommended that the questions are asked in the order presented here, however it is also important to ensure the presentation flows.

### Deliverable: Project deliverables/operationalised CTQ characteristics

- Where, when and how often does the problem occur?
- How severe is the problem?
- What are the key input variables? What are the key process variables? What are the key output variables?
- What are the agreed upon definitions of the high impact characteristics (CTQs), defect(s), unit(s), and opportunities that will figure into the sigma calculations and process capability metrics?

### Deliverable: Performance standard for Project Y

- What is the current process performance in terms of its capability indices, yield or sigma level(s)?
- How large is the gap between current performance and the customer-specified (goal) performance?
- How does work flow through the entire process or operation? Has a workplace map been validated? What did you learn from it?
- What key measures identified indicate the performance of the business process?

### Deliverable: Data collection plan and MSA

- How did the team ensure that it can give usable and reliable data?
- Were the data collectors properly trained?
- How did the team select a sample? Did the team ensure that sampling frequency provided valid representation of the variable being measured?
- What has the team done to assure the stability and accuracy of the measurement process?

### Deliverable: Process capability for Project Y

- Did you manage to identify some of the gaps shown on the "as is" process map? How?
- What does the data say about the performance of the business process?
- How were the process capability indices arrived at? Were the results verified, and validated?

- What were the crucial "moments of truth" on the map?

With the use of a data collection plan that is verified and performed properly, the Sponsor leads the team to determine what the organisation is currently doing, how well (or how badly) they are doing it or how much they are meeting customer satisfaction. In this stage, the Sponsor should remind the team that the main goal of measure activities is to gather as much information from the current process and not to determine how to improve the process.

## The ANALYSE Phase

During the Analyse Phase the team uses systematic analysis to arrive at the root cause of the defects. Analytical tools are used to evaluate whether the identified problem or defect is real and therefore solvable; otherwise, if it is random, it is unsolvable within the Six Sigma framework.

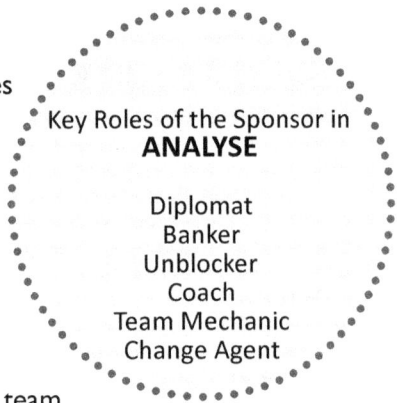

Key Roles of the Sponsor in
**ANALYSE**

Diplomat
Banker
Unblocker
Coach
Team Mechanic
Change Agent

At the start of the Analyse Phase, the team develop an analysis plan that maps out the analysis process and where they document all observations and conclusions from the various studies. The analysis plan ensures that the team is on the right track and that decision-making is based on validated facts.

| Key Steps in the Analyse Phase | Tools/Techniques the Project Team May Use | Typical Project Team Deliverables |
|---|---|---|
| Establish process capability | • Capability Indices<br>• Process Map Review and Analysis<br>• Control Chart | Process capability for Project Y |
| Define performance objectives | • Benchmarking | Improvement goal for Project Y |

| Identify sources of variation and determine root causes | • Histogram<br>• Cause and Effect Diagram<br>• Pareto<br>• Time Series, Run Charts<br>• Scatter Charts<br>• 5 WHYs<br>• Regression Analysis<br>• Statistical Analysis, Normal and/ or Non-normal Data Analysis, Hypothesis Tests<br><br>Lean Tools: Detailed Process Map, 5 WHYs, Value Stream Mapping, Random Input, Reframing Matrix, Conflict Resolution Diagram, Future Reality Diagram | Prioritised list of all Xs |

*Table 2.5 – Steps, Tools and Deliverables in Process Analysis*

There are several statistical techniques that the team could use to understand which factors have the most significant influence on process results. The use of a combination of statistical tools and Lean techniques enhances the validity of information gathered and boosts integrity of decision-making. Sometimes though, progress on the project might stop because of "paralysis by analysis" – this is when the project leader gets lost in the data and investigates hypotheses that aren't relevant to solving the problem. Project Sponsors need to be mindful of this risk to ensure the integrity of analytical inferences and conclusions. The Sponsor could address this problem by ensuring disciplined adherence to the project charter (and if possible statistical methods) by referring to the Master Black Belt for guidance. An irrelevant hypothesis equals wrong solutions equals wasted individual and organisational resources. Although judicious analysis is a must, unbridled data and long-drawn analysis should be avoided to save time and effort. The team should be astute enough to identify "quick wins" that could directly and speedily solve process defects and problems.

The Analysis Phase uncovers the root causes of the problem and suggests ways to address these root causes. If the root causes are not well defined, the team should retrace their steps in the Measure Phase, fix the data collection process, re-gather information and re-analyse additional data.

At the end of the Analyse Phase the team brainstorm solutions to the problem and begin to formulate arguments as to why each proposed improvement would work. The project team usually proposes at least three possible solutions to eliminate the gap between the current state and the desired level of performance.

## What a Sponsor should expect from an Analyse Project Review

The following set of questions should allow the sponsor to get some real clarity and be able to make a decision to allow the project to progress to the next phase. It is recommended that the questions are asked in the order presented here, however it is also important to ensure the presentation flows.

### Deliverable: Relationships and myths

- What are the potential root causes of the gap between where the customer wants performance to be and what the process is actually delivering?
- Were there any cycle time improvement opportunities identified from the process analysis?
- What are the revised rough order estimates of the financial savings/ opportunity for the improvement project?
- Have any assumptions held in the business either been validated or dispelled?

### Deliverable: Root causes

- Which factors turned out to be the root causes of the problem as supported by the team analysis? Can you explain how the root causes were identified?
- How did you know that you arrived at root causes and not symptoms?

- Have you found any "quick wins" or "quick hat" improvements? What is the plan for implementing them?
- Have any additional benefits been identified that will result from closing all or most of the gaps?

### Deliverable: Prioritised list of all Xs

- Has the team prepared a prioritisation matrix?
- What conclusions were drawn from the team's data collection and analysis?
- How did the team reach these conclusions?
- With all additional knowledge, is there a need to change the project charter?

The Sponsor should ensure that the team utilises the data gathered in the Define and Measure Phases to confirm root causes. Careful process analysis through Lean Six Sigma, however, does not only entail identification of root causes of variation but also strives to pinpoint other factors that could adversely affect the process in the future. This new information should be integrated with previous conclusions, and the project purpose and charter should be revised in the light of discovery and hindsight.

The Project Sponsor should ensure disciplined adherence to Six Sigma tools and statistical findings to ensure integrity of the analytical conclusions. He or she should ensure congruence of team efforts and that members do not insulate themselves or immerse themselves in their respective functions.

## The IMPROVE Phase

If the Analyse Phase demonstrates that the problem is real, the next thing the Lean Six Sigma team does is to identify solutions to improve the process based on the data analysis. Success can also be in the form of closing the project at this point as the "myth has been busted", rather than continuing to waste precious company resources for little or no return. For example, a project team working on how to improve the customer satisfaction rating of a call centre company proposed two possible solutions: to shift traffic to the internet or to reduce transfers and callbacks. After a "walk-the-process", it was found that the first solution unduly increased support costs per call so it had to be scrapped.

Key Roles of the Sponsor in **IMPROVE**

Diplomat
Banker
Unblocker
Coach
Team Mechanic
Change Agent

This phase involves determining which proposed solution will best enhance the process within the constraints of available resources. It is during the Improve Phase that a proposed solution is piloted to verify if it works or not.

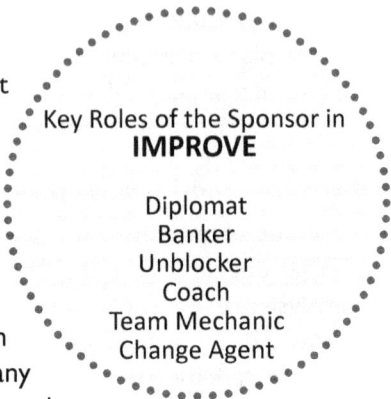

| Key Steps in the Improve Phase | Tools/Techniques the Project Team May Use | Typical Project Team Deliverables |
|---|---|---|
| Carry out designed experiments, screen potential causes, and reduce the number of Xs | • Data Mining<br>• DOE-Fractional<br>• Process Map<br>• Cause and Effect Matrices<br>• QFD/House of Quality<br>• FMEA | List of vital few Xs |
| Discover variable relationships (Xs and CTQs) and propose solutions | • Brainstorming<br>• DOE-Full<br>• Prediction Equations<br>• Cost-Benefit Analysis | Proposed solution |

| Establish operating tolerances of the potential system and check out potential improvement by piloting the proposed solution | • Mistake Proofing/Poka-Yoke<br>• Statistical Tolerancing<br>• Design of Experiments<br>• Pugh Matrix<br>• Simulation Software<br>• QFD<br><br>Lean Tools: Brainstorming, 5S, Visual Factory, Concept Fan, Provocative Operations, Conflict Resolution Diagram, Future Reality Diagram, 5S, Control Error Proofing, Lean Performance Indicator | Piloted solution |

*Table 2.6 – Steps, Tools and Deliverables in Process Improvement*

The last step in the Analyse Phase is usually the first step of the Improve Phase: formulating a list of probable solutions and justifying their feasibility and significance. Through the steps in the Analyse Phase, several process improvement scenarios will be discovered and the project team performs some more analyses to determine which has the best net benefit to the organisation.

Cost-benefit analysis, process experimentation or simulation allows the team to discover the tangible effects of proposed solutions. The team should be mindful of any unintended consequences up or down stream to related processes and the Sponsor must see to it that the team identifies ways to minimise these collateral effects. It is imperative that the Sponsor engage the people who are directly involved in performing a particular task or process being analysed in order to gather insight from their experiences. In fact, in all of the DMAIC phases, the Sponsor should maintain regular communication with the people who are involved in the process sought to be improved. The Sponsor should also ensure that the team has covered off that there are no collateral effects from unintended consequences stemming from the proposed solution.

## What a Sponsor should expect from an Improve Project Review

The following set of questions should allow the sponsor to get some real clarity and be able to make a decision to allow the project to progress to the next phase. There are essentially two stages of the Improve Phase:

1. Generating solutions and selecting the improvement to implement.

2. Piloting and implementing the solution.

### Deliverable: Generating and selecting solutions

- What are the possible solutions suggested by the list of vital few Xs?
- How did the team generate the list of possible solutions?
- Were any criteria developed to assist the team in testing and evaluating potential solutions?
- What criteria were used? How do the criteria relate to the key performance measures?
- How do the proposed solutions remove the key sources of variation discovered in the Analyse Phase?
- Are there any constraints (technical, political, cultural, or otherwise) that would inhibit certain solutions?

### Deliverable: Piloting and implementing the solution

- Was a pilot designed for the proposed solution? What is the design? Has it been tested? How?
- What conclusions were drawn from the outcomes of the pilot?
- What were the underlying assumptions on the cost-benefit analysis?
- Did the team perform mistake-proofing?
- What lessons, if any, from the pilot were incorporated into the design of the full-scale solution?
- Has an implementation plan been developed?
- What does the "should be" process map/design look like?
- What attendant changes will need to be made to ensure that the solution is successful? What was done to address the technical and cultural impact of the changes?
- What best practices can be applied during solution implementation?

- What steps could be taken to manage the cultural and/or political impacts?
- What are the results of the full-scale implementation?
- Have new or revised work instructions resulted? Are they clear and easy to follow?
- What other areas of the organisation can benefit from the new method? How might we get them to adopt the new methods or processes?

At the end of the Improve Phase, the Sponsor should ensure that the team's implementation plan incorporates a change management strategy that will guide the business through the solution implementation and help them adapt to the resulting changes. The Sponsor can facilitate implementation by gaining commitment from key players and maintaining open communication with them.

## The CONTROL Phase

Largely dependent on the success of all the previous phases, the Control Phase allows the project team to set in place control mechanisms for future performance. Success in the Control Phase depends upon how well the team performed in the previous four phases. It is basically the self-checking and self-correcting phase – a Plan/Do/Check/Act cycle.

Key Roles of the Sponsor in
**CONTROL**

Diplomat/Mediator
Banker
Unblocker
Initiator
*Coach*
*Change Agent*

The chief intent of the Control Phase is making the improvements permanent and preventing early deviations from the project's goal. Crucial to the success of the Control Phase is the development of a solid monitoring plan that incorporates appropriate change management strategies and specifies the expectations of the various stakeholders.

After the new procedures are standardised and put in the organisation's documentation system, the team arranges training for the people working in the process and ensures the tools needed to achieve the required standards are met. Once the operational teams are working in the new process, controls are embedded into day-to-day management so that the benefits of the improvements are maintained.

Towards the end of the Control Phase, the Lean Six Sigma project team transfers ownership of the new process to the process owners and all other organisational members responsible for ensuring proper implementation.

| Key Steps | Tools/Techniques the Project Team May Use | Typical Project Team Deliverables |
|---|---|---|
| Standardise the procedures of the approved solution | • Statistical Process Control<br>• Mistake Proofing | Standardise procedure |
| Train participants and all those involved in implementing the solution | • Work-flow Diagrams<br>• Flowcharts<br>• Pareto Charts | Well-trained participants |
| Design control plan | • Operation Analysis Worksheets<br>• Training Manuals | Approved control plan |
| Verify gains and results | • Cost Benefit Analysis | Monitoring plan |
| Document the project | • Process Management Charts<br>• Control Charts | Completed documentation |
| Diffuse the improvements throughout the organisation | Lean Tools: Visual Management, Error Proofing, Current Reality Trees, Conflict Resolution Diagram, Future Reality Diagram, JIT, Transition Tree• | Transfer of ownership |

*Table 2.7 – Steps, Tools and Deliverables in Process Control*

The Sponsor's key role in the Control Phase is to assist the project team in ensuring a solid hand-off of the process from the team to the process owner. When the proposed improvement project is met by resistance as when there are doubts to its immediate value or its sustainability, the Sponsor should assist the project team to provide evidence of sustainability and demonstrate how the organisation can maintain the gains. Failure to communicate information about the new ways of working will result in a perceived lack of immediate value derived from the project.

As the final step of the Control Phase it is worthwhile for the team to conduct a project post-mortem to ensure that future Six Sigma project teams can learn from their experiences.

## What a Sponsor should expect from a Control Project Review

The following set of questions should allow the Sponsor to get some real clarity and be able to make a decision to allow the project to progress to the next phase. It is recommended that the questions are asked in the order presented here, however it is also important to ensure the presentation flows.

### Deliverable: Business ownership

- Who owns the process? Who will own and update documentation? Who will check to make sure that the standard methods or processes are used? How often?
- How will you transfer responsibility for ongoing monitoring to the process owner?
- What other organisational systems, operations, processes, and infrastructures need updates, additions, changes or deletions in order to facilitate knowledge transfer and improvements?
- What other areas of the organisation could adopt and apply the new method?
- What did you learn from the project? To whom should this learning be communicated?
- What is your project closure plan? How will you celebrate your efforts?

### Deliverable: Monitoring

- How will the team or the process owner(s) monitor the implementation plan to see that it is working as intended?

- Was the project goal achieved? How were the original gaps closed?
- How will the process owner and team be able to hold the gains?
- What are the tools and strategies to effectively monitor performance? What action will be taken if the measurements are unsatisfactory?

### Deliverable: 12 months benefits realisation tracking

- What is the team's contingency plan for potential problems during implementation?
- How will the organisation know that the solution worked in 12 months time?
- How will input, process, and output variables be checked to detect sub-optimal conditions?
- How will new or emerging customer needs be identified to ensure the process continues to meet the specifications?

### Deliverable: Standardised procedure

- What is the most recent process yield (or sigma calculation)?
- Does the process performance meet the customer's requirements?
- What are the results of the full-scale implementation, has the improved process and its steps been standardised?
- Are there communication and change management plans to support the implementation of the solution?
- Is there documentation that will support the successful operation of the improvement?
- Does job training on the documented procedures need to be part of the process team's education and training?

The Control Phase goes beyond improvement, and includes the control of the improved process to sustain gains. The Sponsor should see to it that the team conducts continuous monitoring and follow-ups to ensure that the people implementing the improved process are doing it the right way. The Sponsor ensures that monitoring and control are done without let-up and that learning and discovery, although reduced in this phase, will still be performed with enthusiasm. All techniques should still be done with equal rigidity to ensure integrity of results. The Sponsor leads the team to a celebration for a job well done.

3

# Sponsoring and Managing Change

In all my years of working as an engineer and as a Project Sponsor, I have seen that change is the one permanent occurrence in organisations and among people. While change is inevitable, it can also be uncomfortable. In the advent of change, there will be some people who refuse to jump the fence, a few others who willingly take the leap to the other side, and a great many who are astride the fence, without mentioning those who just don't care or are completely clueless. The differences in their reactions create a push-pull effect that maims efforts for meaningful change. With the organisation in disarray, the benefits of the proposed change or process improvement project will be difficult to realise.

Implementing Lean Six Sigma projects is almost always met with resistance and riddled with conflict and anxiety. The Project Sponsor is faced with a plethora of demands and challenges, which are in proportion to the degree of change being sought. Perhaps, the answer to the pervading question – "Why do some projects succeed and why do others fail despite using the same formula?" – is that concomitant ripples of change that permeate the organisation during project implementation could not be kept in check. By failing to do so, roadblocks to change become more intractable and then the situation uncontrollably exacerbates to chaos and conflicts.

It is the Sponsor's ultimate responsibility to be the great unblocker. This chapter presents some concepts of change management, discussed within the framework of Lean Six Sigma and the purview of the Project Sponsor. Later on, in the next chapter, a change management toolkit (8 Cs) for a Project Sponsor is proposed based on the key concepts of change management perspectives.

## Aspects of Change and the People Side of Change

The process of change in Lean Six Sigma has four elements: scale, magnitude, duration, and strategic value.

**Scale:** Does the proposed project affect all or most of the organisation (large-scale) or does it impact only a particular unit or sub-unit of the organisation (small or medium scale)?

**Magnitude:** Will the change result in substantial modifications or minute alterations of the status quo?

**Duration:** Will the project last for one week, one month, one year? How long will the transformation be until the vision of the project is realised?

**Strategic value:** How significant is the outcome of the proposed improvement to business?

Lean Six Sigma projects entail different degrees of change but they always affect three organisational aspects – people, technology and operations. Neglecting to consider one of these aspects could spell project failure, but the most delicate job for a Project Sponsor is managing the people side of change.

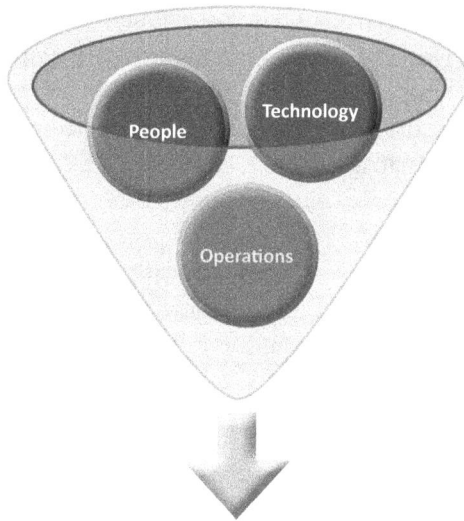

*Figure 3.1 – Aspects of Successful Change*

Relatively, it is easier to control technology and processes than to manage human performance. Human beings are more complicated than technology and processes. Their beliefs, emotions, attitudes, behaviours and tendencies are unpredictable and can be very difficult to manage. Some of the most gruelling roadblocks that a change manager has to deal with are human characteristics – obstinacy, complacency, fear, anger, defiance, pessimism, reluctance and ignorance.

Organisational or process change produces people issues, the most common of which is resistance. David Miller of Changefirst says that resistance to change is a natural human reaction because change disrupts a person's perception of control. Change dislocates us from old habits, from our comfort zones. New things, a new environment, new realities, all evoke a kaleidoscope of feelings and reactions. Anger, resentment, anxiety and sadness are common at different points in the change process.

According to John Kotter, there are basically two types of resistance: systematic and behavioural. Systematic resistance is cognitive in nature and is a product of misunderstanding borne by lack of information, lack of knowledge or lack of skills. Behavioural resistance is emotional in nature and derives from feelings, prejudices, assumptions and beliefs. The behavioural type is the more difficult form of resistance to deal with. Resistance occurs in all levels of the organisation, from the lower ranks to executive management. It is important for change agents to anticipate and respond to people issues, their concerns and feelings, whether they are expressed in terms of practical issues, or emotional responses. Change entails "turbulent transitions" as David Miller terms it. When confronted with change, people often treat it as bad news and harbour feelings of loss and resentment. They usually go through phases of turbulence before settling. This is akin to the cycles of emotional states commonly called the grief cycle which people go through when confronted with loss:

**shock >> denial >> anger >> bargaining >**
**> adapting >> testing >> acceptance**

I call this the *change reaction*. It is inevitable in any type of organisation or in any scale of change. A leader who knows how to spot any of these types of reaction will be able to address them immediately.

**SHOCK:** Disbelief is the first reaction to bad news (*What? I don't believe this!*)

**DENIAL:** They refuse to admit (*This isn't happening. It doesn't make sense!*)

**ANGER:** They get cross (*This is your fault… so frustrating! It's not fair!*)

**BARGAINING:** They try to negotiate (*Please… I promise to up my sales performance. Just don't let me do this!*)

**ADAPTING:** They test the waters (*Well, let me try a bit, see if it's any good.*)

**TESTING:** They taste some more (*Actually, it looks good to me, better than what I usually have!*)

**ACCEPTANCE:** They eat the whole pie (*Oh well… let's move on. I'm in. Let's do that change!*)

At the onset of change, people often ask themselves what they will stand to lose. Feelings of loss and displacement engender anger, discomfort and frustration. While there may be a few who thrive on the challenges of change, people usually, although unconsciously at times, feel threatened and overwhelmed, and adapt to change at a slower pace. Because people have varying degrees of readiness for change (due to differences in knowledge, skills and values), it is often difficult for the change manager to hold the reins and orchestrate a synchronised and well-paced journey from the present to the future.

Human roadblocks to smooth and successful organisational transitions could originate from individuals or from the organisation. Lack of interest, personal aversion to change, distraction, and unwillingness to learn are examples of barriers stemming from the individual. Some forms of organisational barriers are reluctance to assign people or to allocate resources, and negative attitudes towards change. This concept requires a two-pronged change management strategy — one that targets the individual and one that targets the organisation as a whole.

The Change Sponsor has to approach change management from two perspectives – an employee's perspective to manage individual change and a manager's perspective to manage organisational change. As Miller said in his book, *Changefirst*, the people side of change is the most challenging, and successfully implementing change requires matching organisational needs with personal capabilities. Organisational change needs to cascade to the local or individual level. The synergy is depicted in the Changefirst Wheel illustrating the six critical success factors for change management – three for organisational and three for the local level.

Figure 3.2 – The Changefirst Wheel: Six Critical
Success Factors (Miller, 2011)

## Organisational/Program Level:

### Shared Change Purpose

When people in the organisation believe and accept the need for change, they will more likely appreciate and adapt to the proposed change. People need to understand the imperative of change (why change?), the vision (what are the benefits?) and how to go about the change (how to change?). A shared change purpose not only sparks the first steps to change, but it also builds momentum so that the new order of things is sustained and made permanent.

### Effective Change Leadership

Actions speak louder than words. Organisational or project leaders should walk the talk so that they can effectively provide direction, guidance and support for the change especially to those who are responsible for adapting to and implementing the change.

### Powerful Engagement Processes

A change management plan that utilises powerful engagement processes builds commitment, encourages new behaviour and empowers people to develop new knowledge and skills. A powerful engagement process should address involvement of people, learning, rewards and communication. Involvement allows people to discover the need for change and it makes them more committed to it. When people realise that they are given the opportunity to learn how to work in the new way and that adapting to change is properly rewarded, the new order will be easier to galvanise.

## Local or Individual Level:

### Committed Local Sponsors

The middle and front-line managers are the best local sponsors for change in their respective areas of authority. They lead the change and they push the change. Because they are closest to the employees, their working relationship is more personal and they are in the best position to promote a favourable atmosphere to usher in change. Not only are they the most trusted to serve as "sounding boards", local sponsors are also the "buffer" that can give people time to adjust.

### Strong Personal Connection

Strong personal connection to change bolsters personal commitment to the change and allows lasting change. Strengthening personal connection enables people to feel more informed, valued and involved, to regain a sense of control, and to understand the imperatives of change. To personalise the change, a change manager should be able to make people realise that they personally need to change, that the new way is within their capabilities, and that success depends largely on their efforts.

Sustained Personal Performance

The challenges during the transition process should be addressed to ensure that new behaviours continue. In order to sustain personal performance, people should believe that the following factors relating to their job will remain the same or may even be enhanced as a result of change:

- Future security
- Financial impact
- Work relationships
- Level of responsibility
- Learning curve

Applying the Changefirst Wheel to the level of the Project Sponsor, I propose that change implementation should be prepared well, managed skilfully and reinforced relentlessly. Preparing for change allows the Project Sponsor to create a high-level management strategy; managing change requires the merging of the organisational change management strategy with individual change management activities and addressing resistance; and reinforcing change allows the Project Sponsor to assess initial results, identify loopholes and problems, and rectify them.

When guiding the members of the Lean Six Sigma team, the Sponsor should ensure that each member develops the following aspects:

1. An awareness and appreciation of the need for change.
2. The desire to get involved in the transition processes.
3. The knowledge and the skills to undergo change.
4. The determination to sustain the change.

When these are in place, the turbulence may be more effectively managed. As the role models and the buffers for change, Project Sponsors need to engage themselves in the change process. They must undergo change themselves before they can lead. Frequently, we would see leaders eloquently justifying the need for change and how it can benefit the organisation and its people, but by judging their actions, you'd realise their message is – "Change is good. You go first." In contrast, an effective leader says – "Change is good. I go first."

## Undergoing Change Before Leading Change

Project leaders, organisational leaders and change managers should be able not only to demonstrate a theoretical understanding of change but also an active and sincere commitment to undergo the change process. To be successful, change managers have to undergo change themselves before they can lead employees through the transition.

Senior managers need to understand that intellectually they have bought into the change straight away. By initiating the change, Sponsors have usually visualised the future state but they also need to allow themselves the time and freedom to go through the emotional cycle of change. This process tends to be slower than the intellectual analysis, and many Sponsors can find this frustrating.

Downsizing will always be unpleasant to both workers and leadership and when it comes to it, the parting can be painful for some. A senior manager attempting to instil change into a credit team by downsizing, intellectually liked the fact that it would improve his key KPIs. However, he hadn't allowed himself enough time to go through the emotional journey of the impact of downsizing his team. Therefore when it came to it, he was uncomfortable with the way it was done. That discomfort was also felt by the team. Performance suffered and he did not meet his KPIs.

For a Project Sponsor to properly understand the nature of change and its impact on individuals and on organisational groups, he or she must also be able to identify his or her personal perceptions and concerns to map out how best to support and participate in the change. Adapting to change should also be followed with a desire to acquire the skills and knowledge to manage change at the individual and organisational levels. Before the Sponsor can lead people to go through the change process, he or she must first intensify awareness of the need for change. A good change management strategy also considers individual differences in formulating an action plan to harness desire, knowledge and ability of the employees. Feedback mechanisms, performance audits and corrective actions are a must in institutionalising change and making it a corporate culture. Recognising, rewarding and celebrating successes are also necessary to build on the successes.

To successfully kick off a Lean Six Sigma initiative, Project Sponsors should motivate people to not only follow their example but also to embrace their vision. An effective change management plan successfully mitigates risks and barriers to change and reinforces Six Sigma behaviours at all levels of the organisation.

To be an effective change leader, one has to have mastered personal responsibility and accountability. When others perceive you to be willing to admit responsibility for decisions, they will be encouraged to be held accountable for their own choices and actions. When a leader is able to successfully gain consensus on the project goal, he or she is able to instil a sense of ownership among them. Accepting the vision at the start of a Lean Six Sigma project goes a long way to ensuring understanding of what needs to change and why. This is akin to a business practice called Take Ownership and Follow Up (TOFU).

TOFU stresses that ownership follows empowerment, commitment follows ownership, accountability follows commitment, and engagement follows accountability. When people are empowered to have a voice in improvement goals, they assume ownership of the goal and a stake in the outcome. When they feel more in control, they feel more responsible in making changes work. Simply, people buy in when they are involved.

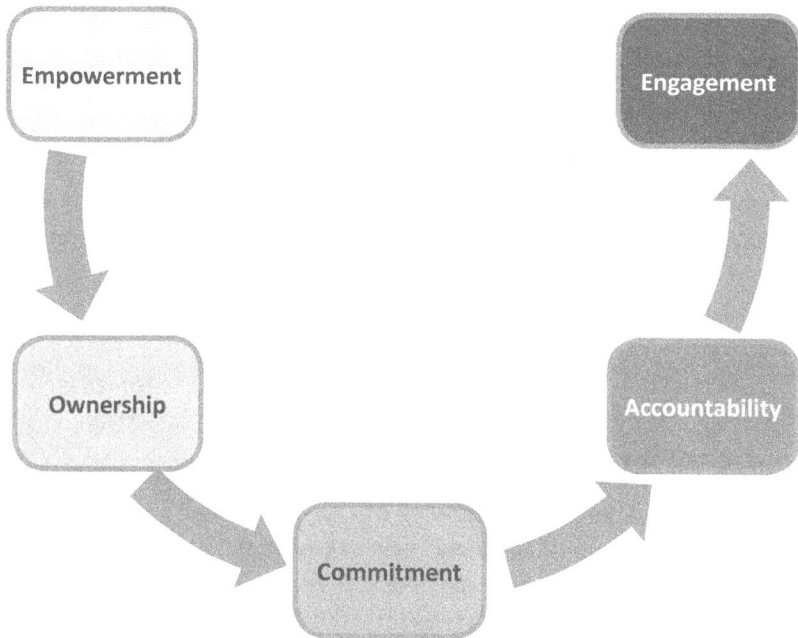

*Figure 3.3 – Getting from Empowerment to Engagement*

An important ingredient of TOFU is that vision must not be imposed. The Sponsor must ensure acceptance and ownership by convincing the business, sometimes painstakingly, of the benefits of the project. Ownership of a vision, a process, a plan, or a project should be one of the crucial subjects that the Project Sponsor must always discuss in his professional relationship with the team members and with the entire organisation, especially the key stakeholders.

Practically, this means a Project Sponsor should:

- Develop a change vision for Lean Six Sigma and motivate members to take ownership of the vision

- Establish a network of support or influencers – a group with enough influence and commitment to actively engage in the change efforts

- Determine the bottlenecks and constraints — those structures and groups resistant to change

- Initiate broad based action to change behaviours through intensive communication and modelling by the influencers

- Identify performance improvements, advertise those wins, reward accomplishments and associate Lean Six Sigma to organisational behaviours

- Leverage on increased credibility to motivate broader support

- Based on knowledge gained, keep updating tactical change management strategies to sustain both team and organisational effectiveness

Academic literature is rich with change management theories and models to enrich a manager's understanding of change. Project Sponsors should remember that there is no single recipe to solve all the problems in any change process because each project consists of different activities and no two individual employees are exactly the same. There is no "one-size-fits-all" approach to managing change. There are however key elements that should underpin any change management strategy.

A roadmap that has been proven to work has two discrete elements of what to do and then how to do it. Effectively, I have formulated this recipe as the 8 Cs framework.

## The 8 Cs Framework: A Toolkit for Sponsoring

The Sponsor should observe four fundamental principles when they guide a Lean Six Sigma project team: clarity, criticality, commitment and consistency. I consider these as the 4 WHATs of sponsoring change. The sponsor must then utilise four strategic tools to deliver and sustain transformative efforts: charter, change, coaching, and communication. These are the 4 HOWs of Lean Six Sigma sponsoring.

| WHATs | HOWs |
|---|---|
| Clarity | Charter |
| Criticality | Change |
| Commitment | Coaching |
| Consistency | Communication |

## The idea in a nutshell

### Clarity

Project goals, performance standards and expectations, procedures, roles and responsibilities should be compellingly clear to increase understanding and acceptance of the project imperatives.

### Criticality

A sense of urgency should be established. The project should link strategy to organisational vision and this can be done by aligning business issues, priorities, processes and metrics. Criticality helps eradicate complacency and engages critical attention to project imperatives.

### Commitment

Nurturing commitment creates passion for success, intensifies dedication and focus, builds both personal capability and team effectiveness, sustains energy and motivation, and builds the infrastructure of accountability.

### Consistency

Observing consistency in the tangible and intangible aspects of project management builds trust, fosters constancy to purpose, strengthens commitment and dispels unpredictability and myths.

### Charter

A good project charter sets direction and focus, keeps the project team on track, effectively monitors progress, nurtures a sense of ownership of the project, renders legitimacy, and compels (or encourages) responsibility and accountability.

### Change

A good change management plan serves as a Sponsor's bible in anticipating as well as introducing change, and negotiating the problematic road from project planning to implementation.

### Coaching

Coaching boosts self-esteem, confidence and competence; helps team members achieve peak performance; removes roadblocks caused by resistance to change; develops team unity; promotes individual and team excellence. A good coaching plan enables the Sponsor to address the concerns of both individuals and the team as a whole.

### Communication

A good communication plan facilitates effective and efficient communications with all the people involved in the project including the stakeholders. It is a tool that harnesses the other 7 Cs.

How these elements align with Miller's Changefirst Wheel of Critical Success Factors may be illustrated in this manner:

| Changefirst Wheel | 8 Cs Framework | |
|---|---|---|
| Critical Success Factor | WHATs | HOWs |
| 1. Shared change purpose | Clarity<br>Criticality<br>Commitment | Charter<br>Change<br>Communication |
| 2. Effective change leadership | Clarity<br>Criticality<br>Commitment<br>Consistency | Change<br>Communication |
| 3. Powerful engagement processes | Commitment<br>Consistency | Change<br>Coaching<br>Communication |
| 4. Committed local sponsors | Commitment<br>Consistency | Charter<br>Change<br>Communication |

| 5. Strong personal connection | Commitment | Change |
|---|---|---|
| | Criticality | Coaching |
| | Consistency | Communication |
| 6. Sustained personal performance | Commitment | Change |
| | Consistency | Coaching |
| | | Communication |

This **8 Cs** framework gives focus to the Sponsor's efforts to lead the Lean Six Sigma team to project success. The Sponsor may opt to apply one or a combination of change management approaches. Whatever the decision, they can use the **8 Cs** as a toolkit to hone their chosen strategy, repair its loopholes or make up for its weaknesses.

# The WHATs of Sponsoring

The previous chapters have concentrated on the stage gates for Lean Six Sigma and change management generally. A short introduction of the 8 Cs of sponsoring change explained that these constitute great leadership actions for management and more specifically for driving business improvement in Lean Six Sigma and change management. The tools that can be used by the Sponsor to pursue these actions are explained in the next chapter.

## 1. Clarity

> *"Effective leaders don't have to be passionate. They don't have to be charming. They don't have to be brilliant… They don't have to be great speakers. What they must be is clear. Above all else, they must never forget the truth that of all the human universals – our need for security, for community, for clarity, for authority, and for respect – our need for clarity… is the most likely to engender in us confidence, persistence, resilience, and creativity." – Marcus Buckingham (The One Thing You Need to Know:…About Great Managing, Great Leading, and Sustained Individual Success, Free Press, 2005)*

Perhaps, the most potent argument for clarity is that if we are not clear about a problem, then we can't fix it. If we do not understand a plan, we can't implement it. When we are uncertain of what we are trying to achieve, we can't get there. Lack of clarity in the components of a

Lean Six Sigma project is antithetical to the principles of Lean Six Sigma because uncertainties and ambiguities waste time and resources.

For the Lean Six Sigma Sponsor, if they are not clear about the benefits of a process improvement project, they cannot sell it (to the organisational leaders, process owners and their project team). Real clarity is when the problem or opportunity of the project can be articulated in one to two sentences without using significant inclusion of acronyms, using simple language to avoid ambiguity.

I worked with a Sponsor who has a PhD and over 25 years' experience in the business. He presented to me his problem statement as part of the charter. He explained the problem for over 10 minutes, with great detail and many acronyms. To be honest, I understood the general principle of his project but he lost me on why the project was so urgent. He explained each of the 71 significant injuries in the business over the previous year. So I asked him if he had explained to his 11-year-old daughter the way he had explained it to me, would she have really understood. He stopped and then answered "No", so he tried again, but after 5 minutes I interrupted him again and reminded him to imagine talking to his daughter and how he would make her grasp the significance of the project.

I stressed the simple rule: unravel the COMPLEX, make it SIMPLE and then make it COMPELLING. He took the COMPLEX and made it SIMPLE – "There were basically 71 serious injuries to our staff or contractors in the last 12 months." This was making it SIMPLE. But to really drive the CRITICALITY of the project in the minds of employees, he had to make it really COMPELLING. He came up with – "We injure on average 1 person every 5 days," then added, "compared to industry standard of 42 days." He further added: "Any delays in finding and implementing solutions would on average result in a major injury every 5 days." This made it URGENT.

The Project Sponsor and all of the members of the Six Sigma team should have a succinct understanding of the problem, the solution and the roadmap towards success. Clarity requires that there is a clear alignment and correlation between project goals, performance standards, individual responsibilities, review processes and control systems. To achieve clarity, the Project Sponsor should ensure that goals, standards and responsibilities, as well as success indicators, are understood throughout the organisation.

Clarity should be maintained for the whole duration of the project and not only at the beginning. A Sponsor should be quick to identify signs of doubts and uncertainties.

"I thought…"

"I missed the point…"

"I'm not sure if…"

"I just don't get it."

"We did it this way the last time…"

"I suppose we may…"

"Most likely…"

"Probably…"

It may be naïve to say that a Sponsor can anticipate or immediately spot signs of unclearness and ambiguities at all times, but he or she must take whatever steps are necessary to erase doubts right at the onset of the project. The rule is to avoid vagueness as much as possible even when vagueness is unavoidable.

A Project Sponsor should explain the imperatives of a Lean Six Sigma project in vivid terms. Clear alignment of project goals helps ensure the project team are all working towards the same outcome and reduces confusion, which can often result in instability, lack of accountability, poor performance, negative outcomes, and failure. To develop clarity, the Sponsor should:

- Set clear organisational priorities and realistic project objectives and link them to the Lean Six Sigma roadmap and strategy

- Clarify roles and responsibilities of the team members, the executive management, and other stakeholders and ensure acceptance of the project team ground rules

- Maintain an effective organisational communications plan

- Reconcile conflicting personalities and priorities

- Distil any threat that leads to confusion

For the Sponsor, clarity is the first step to gaining credibility and respect, and also to stamping the project with legitimacy so that the team can embrace the shared purpose more readily.

### Chef Analogy for Clarity:

The kitchen is the most chaotic part of the restaurant. Yet with an experienced chef who skilfully manages the kitchen staff, it always seems like they all move with speed and precision, with each one knowing what to do at the precise moment, and knowing exactly what is in their station. A good chef ensures that everyone is clear on their respective tasks. Another important role of the chef is to communicate clearly with the customers the essence of each of the dishes and the main intent of the menu, to represent the restaurant.

## 2. *Criticality*

*"A false sense of urgency is pervasive and insidious because people mistake activity for productivity… a sense of urgency is not an attitude that I must have the project team meeting today but that the meeting must accomplish something important today." – John Kotter (A Sense of Urgency)*

The dictionary defines criticality as "the quality, state, or degree of being of the highest importance." In business operations or in financial terms, criticality describes the ranking of the severity of the various ways in which a system, device, or process can fail, their frequency of occurrence, and the consequences of their failure. The purpose of this ranking is to guide organisations in choosing which battles to wage first.

I have had many Sponsors who find difficulty in driving the criticality of the project, or as John Kotter refers to as "a sense of urgency". As businesses in my experience have a wide array of opportunities and are constrained only by the availability of critical resources and people to deliver them, I always remind the project team to stress to senior management why the project has to be PRIORITISED over others and how the expected outcomes work to achieve organisational objectives. In short, I encourage them to issue a sort of a warning like: there is a typhoon coming; it is big, it is strong; if nobody listens, if nobody does anything about it, we will have another Katrina. This is true, but I believe that "fire-fighting" is endemic amongst most senior managers. That is they are prepared to let something fail before they fix it.

For Lean Six Sigma projects to be successful, it is important to understand why the organisation decided to pursue the initiative. However, a more important concern should deal with the sense of urgency – "the organisation should do it NOW, otherwise..." Kotter asserts that "underlying a true sense of urgency is a set of feelings: a compulsive determination to *move and win, now.*" And because feelings are more influential than thoughts, melodramatic stories highlighting the urgency are digested with more interest and are embedded in us far longer than would high level presentations or any overly technical explanations.

Driving urgency is making the purpose of a project compelling. However, the Sponsor often discovers that what is compelling to him or her may not be compelling to others and that what motivates him or her may not necessarily motivate others. According to Karen Nelson, storytelling is the safest way to make people aware of a problem that impedes change and of the consequences when it is ignored. Stories have the unique ability to place issues in context and can vividly portray cause and effect. However, not just one story could draw out that "Eureka!" Hence, part of a Sponsor's leadership arsenal should be a collection of stories that sends different messages and elicits different reactions and behaviours. Project Sponsors can even use personal stories professionally to make the organisation accept that a situation is critical.

Driving a sense of urgency has a number of facets, firstly how to get the team to really understand the priority and importance of the project and also to get the rest of the stakeholders to agree on this criticality. It is relatively simple in organisations that have a project management office that uses a robust prioritisation methodology agreed by everyone. The challenge is in organisations that exact compliance to preset priorities and this manifests itself in managers' pet projects overtaking company or divisional/department priorities that are more urgent. This redounds to confusion among employees who are in the know and who by experience discover more pressing realities. The Sponsor should guard against this confusion and not having clarity on the specific criticality of the project/ initiative. It is important for the Sponsor to be really clear on why the project is important and about its linkage to the business strategy, and do this in a succinct way.

The following are the three basic questions that the Sponsor should ask team members:

1.   Why is this project more important than all the others/my day job?

2.   Why do this project right now?

3.   What happens if we do nothing?

Key to driving the business case is the ability to take the COMPLEX business situation/problem/opportunity and then boil it down to its core item, i.e. make it SIMPLE. This is quite often a pivotal question that really answered would irrevocably address the aim of the project or initiative. This ability to make it succinct and simple is an iterative process and can take a few hours or even days to get right.

This brings me onto the second point around selling the criticality of the project or change – taking the SIMPLE and making it COMPELLING. Just because a senior manager says something, does not make it compelling.

He must have the ability to sell it in the form of a "story". There is a very simple recipe to help sell the criticality that is against usual management consultancies' approach of telling the answer first then selling it as the correct answer. I find this method very effective in making my message both clear and compelling. This process can be done in the following manner:

1. State the current situation the business is facing, e.g. losing market share. Put only the positives from a SWOT analysis in here. State the entity in question, the aim/mission of the project or initiative, and any preset objectives (e.g. x% growth in the next 12 months, minimise capital expenditure requirement, etc.).

2. List all the facts and sort them into like groupings relevant to the situation being discussed and put aside irrelevant data.

3. Interpret these groupings and add a sentence – "So what?"

4. Collate the consequences – these can come from the WOT of a SWOT analysis.

5. Create a consequence chain, i.e. consequence of doing nothing is A and the consequence of A is B; consequence B produces C which in turn results in consequence D, and so on. Then identify root causes – this can come from the analysis phase of a Lean Six Sigma project.

6. Iterate the key or pivotal question and evaluate if the answer really accesses the aim of the project or change.

7. Give the answer.

8. Give the solutions/recommendations with the supporting data.

Following this structure tells a story and makes the sell COMPELLING. A simpler way to look at this process is to proceed by addressing a series of 5 questions:

1. Where are we today?

2. What needs addressing?

3.    What question do we need to answer?

4.    How and when are we going to do it?

5.    Why? (Provide evidence)

To assess the criticality of a certain project, the Lean Six Sigma team must position the vision for the project amidst the spectrum of business challenges, trends and issues. The Project Sponsor should be able to stir the team to examine market and competitive realities and then identify and dissect challenges, potential crises and opportunities. But this is not enough. To create buy-in for a project, the Sponsor should target not only the minds but also the hearts of people. Since it is people who are the most problematic factor in successfully transitioning organisational processes, Sponsors should aim at feelings and attitudes. The organisation needs to grab great opportunities whenever possible and to nurture, as Kotter said, "a compulsive determination to move, and win, now."

To put criticality into action, the Sponsor should:

- Establish a sense of urgency
- Identify what is critical (urgent) from among the wide array of important organisational goals and values
- Clarify project prioritisation relative to other organisational initiatives
- Leverage organisational Lean Six Sigma capability by reinforcing purposes and processes
- Cover all bases by comprehending all that can be known and minimising what is unknown

A lack of urgency is one of the reasons why organisational transformation fails. Without a sense of urgency, people become complacent, processes stagnate, and problems complicate. Complacency paralyses corporate time and becomes the ingredient of failure. The Project Sponsor must therefore emphasise not only what is crucial but also what is urgent, why it is urgent, and how to address the urgency.

**Chef Analogy for Criticality:**

The chef will always determine the balance of quality/consistency and time to delivery. Clear communications exist in the kitchen on getting the dish out on time, every time, and then consistently reinforcing the sense of urgency to get the dish out on time to meet the customers' expectations.

## 3. Commitment

*"The harder you work, the harder it is to surrender." – Vincent Lombardi (American football coach)*

Commitment, as the dictionary would describe, is "the trait of sincere and steadfast fixity of purpose or that state of being bound emotionally or intellectually to a course of action or to another person or persons." Commitment to a project (including its vision, objectives, activities, and requirements) would then mean belief and acceptance of the project, translated to a willingness to exert considerable effort to achieve purposes and objectives, and a desire to keep working for the group until completion.

A Project Sponsor came to me to seek advice about how he should go about getting his people to "buy into" some Lean Six Sigma proposals. I told him he could go barge in through the front door or creep his way in via the back entrance. Going through the front door would allow him to visibly demonstrate his vision and actively engage his staff in project planning and implementation. If he decides to take the backdoor, he will be relegated to the role of a silent or invisible initiator, policing the changes behind the scenes. He opted for first alternative (which of course is the right thing to do).

Had he opted for the latter, he would have failed to grab that singular opportunity to build buy-in, keep the team on track and sustain commitment to the project. Active involvement by the Sponsor allowed him to explain the rationale and the expected benefits of the project which lent clarity and legitimacy. Had he chosen back end management, he would have garnered the support and commitment of one or two of his friendly supporters rather than capturing the whole team. When he is out of action, a Sponsor is not able to engage the team from exhausting possible solutions to a problem. Choosing the path of the silent leader, the Sponsor would have been limited to speaking only in abstract terms. Put simply, he would have failed to optimise all the opportunities to maximise project success.

A Project Sponsor should set the stage for successful project execution by actively demonstrating confidence, commitment and focus on the Lean Six Sigma initiative. Commitment encourages the team members to maximise their skills and utilise their discretionary energies to learn new things, utilise new tools, and implement new approaches which will ultimately enhance collective skill and team ambition.

However, commitment does not only entail dedicated focus to the Lean Six Sigma project, but also requires the leader's commitment to human needs. A Project Sponsor must show loyalty to individual welfare because the members can only trust him or her to the degree to which he or she is committed to individual integrity and well-being. The Sponsor can do this by:

- Showing focus, dedication and intensity in all the phases of the project

- Developing a team-building plan to harness both heart and mind of team members

- Modelling high trust behaviours

- Showing accountability and admitting culpability

- Recognising and promoting integrity and well-being of team members

In one company I worked with, each Sponsor was asked to gather feedback from their team and their Master Black Belt on their performance as a Sponsor. One Sponsor came to me very frustrated about the feedback he had from the team and said he needed to discuss the issue as he saw it, so that he could review objectively and not hold negative feelings or resentments. One comment said that the team did not feel that his (Sponsor's) commitment to the project was very high. This was extremely disappointing to him as he was the one that had come up with the idea for the project. He had written the original draft and had given some of his team's time to work through the project, and then supported the process from roll out to implementation to follow up. "How dare they question my commitment?" he blurted.

I asked him a few questions. Firstly, what was his definition of commitment? He said, "I showed my commitment by fully supporting the team, giving them advice and money, answering their questions, and making decisions. What more did they want?" I then asked him what he thought the team definition of commitment was. He answered, the same as his, of course. So to the third question, did he ask the team what their expectations were of him as a Sponsor at the beginning or anytime during the project? A rather sheepish "No" came as the reply. We agreed that he should try to do two things:

1.  Go back to the team and ask them, in an authentic and non-threatening manner, how he could show his VISIBLE commitment for his next project at the wrap up and lessons learnt meeting during Control Phase.

2.  Talk to one or two of his peers that gave positive feedback in the area of commitment and ask how he could strengthen even further what were deemed as his strong points.

I caught up with him a few weeks later and he was really positive about this newly acquired skill, i.e. eliciting commitment from others and showing personal commitment. He had started rolling it out not only for his next big project that he was just launching, but also to the everyday management of his team. He said there were a few more simple things that he observed were making a difference to his whole leadership: responding to the needs of his team both big and small, regular reporting and monitoring, constantly articulating the visions and objectives with clarity, and helping them understand the importance and priority or as Kotter put it a sense of urgency. A very interesting point is how he reframed the essence of Voice of the Customer: he treated his team members as if they were his customers, since he was providing them a management/leadership service. He needed to get a VOC initially and then kept on checking in just in case their needs changed. In his new project, he attended the first launch meeting but tried to make time to attend a number of team meetings and then also ensured that he caught up every two weeks with the Black Belt even for just 15 minutes, sometimes only by phone. These were indeed very visible ways to show his commitment and enthusiastic support to the project and to his team.

Interestingly, this particular Sponsor's performance in the employee survey seven months later was the highest ever in the division's history and 9% higher than any other manager.

My idea of putting commitment to work is akin to Collin Powel's argument in his book, *My American Journey,* that "Perpetual optimism is a force multiplier." A leader's enthusiasm, his "we can do it" attitude, resonates through the entire project team. But even a small cry of exasperation or cynicism could send deafening echoes to a team that is already overwhelmed with all the new and strange things that they have to contend with.

An organisation that inspires commitment among its members breeds a passion for success. A leader gains commitment to a shared change purpose and energises the team into action and engagement through visible commitment. Sponsors must remember that the level of commitment and the intensity they demonstrate will resonate with the members of the project team and stimulate similar behaviour.

## Chef Analogy for Commitment:

The chef has to don an apron from time to time to show her staff what should be done and how it should be done, especially when she has just introduced a new item to the menu or a new procedure in the kitchen.

Checking with her kitchen staff regularly ensures that every dish that is delivered out of the kitchen through the staff to the table of every single diner meets customer satisfaction whether she is in the kitchen or not.

## 4. Consistency

*"Make your mold. The best flux in the world will not make a usable shape unless you have a mold to pour it in." – Robert Collier (American motivational author, 1885–1950)*

You just had a great kick-off meeting with your project team, a signal that the project is off to a great start. Everyone was excited about the project. Each team member was clear about what needs to be done, how to do it and when to do it. After a few days, you take out your checklist and make a cursory evaluation of what has been accomplished so far. To your horror and dismay, not a single box contains a tick mark! No one touched or moved anything! If you ask why, you will realise your team has stumbled on a number of roadblocks. If this can happen at the start of a project, it can very well happen in the middle and even toward the end.

In each stage of the project, there will always be constraints and unexpected events that bear on the ability to perform such that team momentum and synergy is effectively curtailed. You will realise that these stumbling blocks did not all arise from the team members. Many project constraints are caused by executive leaders or organisational occurrences. The importance of consistency right from beginning to end comes to the fore. It is through consistency of efforts and boundless synergy that the project team is able to hurdle the humps and to sidetrack or negotiate events that divert focus. The Project Sponsor has to quickly restore the team and prompt them again to the urgency of the job at hand. Don't waste time. Don't wait for the team to rebound on its own. Don't look to management to do your job for you.

It is important that a leader shows consistency between his or her words and his or her deeds. It is walking the talk. Given that a successful Lean Six Sigma initiative requires roadmaps, tools and methods to have been used correctly, Project Sponsors who embrace and strongly espouse the Lean Six Sigma principles will more quickly gain the trust of the project team.

Consistency builds trust, trust builds commitment, commitment draws support, support nurtures attitude, attitude bolsters synergy, synergy enhances success. In this sense, consistency becomes the most pragmatic element of Lean Six Sigma endeavours. As a charismatic leader, the Project Sponsor who consistently expresses their values for Lean Six Sigma generates a shared value in the project team.

When I coach Sponsors, I never fail to emphasise that they should always imagine themselves as being on stage, the centre of attention, the source of inspiration, the prompt for decision-making and action. Thus, as a Sponsor, you have to mean what you say, and do what you mean. You have to be "predictable" in the sense that the audience will not for one second doubt your belief and adherence to the Lean Six Sigma project. They know of your commitment to Lean Six Sigma and know how you'd decide. They know what you want and what you believe is how things should be done. Imagine again if every morning or on every occasion that you are meeting the group, they will wonder what kind of Sponsor will enter the door.

Will it be deadbeat, indifferent Mr Do-What-You-Want-Bore?

Will it be the livid Mr Do-Nothing-Big-Boss?

Will it be the Mr Pretending-To-Be-Busy-Guy?

Will it be the animated Mr Let's-Do-It-Go-Getter?

Consistency is tangible evidence of authenticity and integrity, thus is the most effective way to build one's professional brand and value proposition as a Sponsor, in fact, it is the surest way to sell yourself to your boss and to your workforce. Consistency is how the Sponsor gains respect and trust from above him or her, and from below. If you have a "now you see, now you don't" attitude to the project, your people will not be able to grasp your true intentions, they will not know where you are coming from. And when this happens, fear of the uncertain will creep in the team, or worse, everybody will be led to believe that he or she can do whatever they want to do in any which way they can. But when you consistently show up, speak up, and own up, you are able to set the tone and tenor of work standards and expectations, hence you help the group create consensus, avoid confusions and maintain project direction.

The Sponsor will demonstrate consistency and thereby enhance the project's likelihood of success by doing the following:

- Constantly express support to Six Sigma philosophy and values

- Show consistency between words and deeds

- Create a coherent and continuous system of identifying and linking opportunities, core processes and Six Sigma roadmap

- Ensure consistent monitoring of project details and milestones

- Design a scoreboard to highlight successes, analyse failures and diagnose strengths and weaknesses

When he or she is able to do these, the Project Sponsor creates the mould where the productive energies of their team come into shape and are galvanised into fruition and resilience.

## Chef Analogy for Consistency:

A newly hired chef saw the potential of making use of local ingredients which are abundant in the locale of the business but otherwise rarely used because they are seen to be common and therefore not exotic and not expensive. Her staff were appalled, envisaging they might lose their VIP customers. At first, only a handful tried the chef's new recipes. But the chef never relented in selling the idea to her people, to the diners, and to the big boss. She showed enthusiasm, never impatience or frustration, in how to prepare the food and how to savour it. She never wavered until a Hollywood star who tried the dish said on Twitter and Facebook how foie gras with ginger and mango smelt and tasted so good. The chef capitalised on this – published it in the local daily and celebrated the win with her team.

Clarity, Criticality, Commitment, and Consistency is a doable paradigm that provides the signposts for Sponsors in the performance of their job. You are free to throw in one or more other Cs into the soup but these 4 Cs should be taken as key ingredients. How to deliver these 4 WHAT Cs and how to make them work effectively relies on a set of strategies – the HOWs of sponsoring change and improvement projects.

# 5

# The HOWs of Sponsoring Change

*Chapter 4* has spelt out the actions, or WHATs, a sponsor should do. This chapter builds on the tools, or the HOWs, to deliver the WHATs. These actions are built around a second set of 4 Cs – Charter, Change, Coaching, and Communication.

## 1. *Charter*

*"If we are facing in the right direction, all we have to do is keep on walking."*
*– Buddhist Proverb*

The project charter has been sufficiently discussed in *Chapter 2* as being one of the key deliverables in the Define Phase. This section will expound a little on the importance of having a charter.

The development of a well-conceived project charter is one of the first requirements of any Lean Six Sigma initiative. The project charter is a guidance document that serves as the project team's compass and rudder. Agreement among those involved is necessary to avoid confusion and complacency. When all are in agreement of what the project aims to achieve and how these goals are to be accomplished, the project charter becomes a covenant for engagement. It is akin to a binding contract, a sort of a conscience document which compels the performance of obligations.

The charter is the pivotal document that acts as the contract between the Sponsor and the project leader. I coach Sponsors to push back if they see a problem statement that is a few paragraphs or pages long. This is a signal that the project leader is not really sure of the focus of the project. In an instance like this, the Sponsor should ask the 11-year-old test question, or ask the team to summarise the project statement in two sentences. As a Sponsor you have to be able to, or get the belt to, articulate the problem statement in two sentences, ask them to describe the process in 5 – 7 steps in the SIPOC.

In my years of working with many Sponsors and organisations, I have actively promoted the use of a one page charter, as senior managers don't really have the time to read many pages.

There are three questions every project manager and Sponsor MUST answer:

1.  What is the problem or opportunity being addressed/fixed by the project (in two sentences)?

2.  What is the scope, i.e. what will be fixed and what will not be fixed/ changed by the project?

3.  How will you measure project success?

Every project leader that has come to training I have run, either for Lean Six Sigma or project management, struggles in answering these three questions and has to go back to their Sponsor for clarification and approval since both project team and Sponsor have to concur. A great question for the Sponsor to ask is: "Would you be happy to have these project goals as part of your annual performance review to determine your pay rise/bonus?" Once the Sponsor treats the charter as a contract between them and the project leader/team, they tend to treat it with more respect.

I have often seen Sponsors who assume that the charter is set in stone upfront and are afraid to change it once it is written down and signed off in the initial phases. This lamentably locks the project down and compromises real and meaningful improvements.

Project charters in Lean Six Sigma initiatives should be allowed to evolve as more data and analysis become available, and in particular as scope and measures of success are qualified. However, for pure project management projects, changes to timing and scope have to be formally signed off as deviations incurring costs. All projects require scope/timing changes to be signed off at project reviews.

Over the years, I have added items to the list of common project charter flaws:

- There is a solution already predicated in the problem/opportunity statement. The key role of the Sponsor is to only articulate the problem being addressed and not pre-empt a solution.

- The goals contain pure benefits and do not specify leading measures to determine project progress, success and sustainability, e.g. total dollars earned/saved rather than reduction of the unit cost per item or increase of number of items per sale.

- Scope has nothing listed as being out of scope, the charter should specify anything reasonable in out of scope so that stakeholders understand what is not going to be addressed.

- Quite often, resources are allocated as percentages of their time, e.g. 20%. This means that resources tend not to be able to dedicate their time to the project. The Sponsor needs to confirm which day/half days they will dedicate to the project and confirm with the manager of that resource.

- Long project charters for projects tend to become project specifications rather than a succinct summary of the project. The charter should be brief but sufficiently broad and clear to cover the basic elements.

- For general projects, including Lean Six Sigma, few Belts are able to really articulate measures of success and to say the project is complete.

It is worthwhile to reiterate that the Project Sponsor should ensure that the charter provides an appropriate project goal and a project scope that is congruent to the company's resources and capabilities. The Sponsor should also ensure that a project tracking system is incorporated for evaluation and replication purposes.

However, the project charter is not a cure-all document. It cannot provide solutions to all problems that occur throughout the project. It is when such problems occur that the Sponsor initiates actions for the revision of the charter. He or she approves changes in the team charter or in the project scope as may be necessary. Project Sponsors should make sure the project team:

- Gathers data prior to drafting the project charter

- Clearly articulates incremental project deliverables, milestones and completion aligned to strategic objectives

- Carefully estimates strategic, organisational or financial impact and optimises key project attributes (e.g. duration, geography and cross functionality)

- Secures agreement from team members and stakeholders to manage expectations

- Allows revisions as new learning and knowledge arise

Most importantly, the Sponsor should always bear in mind that organisational charts, project plans and charters are frozen inanimate components of a project. They don't move by themselves and do not accomplish anything by themselves. It is only when the people component of the project begins to move that these objects come to life. The Sponsor may well be guided by change management principles, effective coaching and excellent communication skills to bring life to the actionable steps in the project charter.

## Chef Analogy for Charter:

The chef provides direct boundaries of each of the dishes to table staff through what each dish consists of and also how much it will cost. This helps manage expectations and minimise customer dissatisfaction and disputes. With the proliferation of allergies, it is important to manage the business risk and help provide information supply to customers so they can make a decision on which dishes to order.

## 2. Change

> *"Change is hard because people overestimate the value of what they have*
> *– and underestimate the value of what they may gain by giving that up." –*
> *James Belasco and Ralph Stayer (Fight of the Buffalo, 1994)*

Change is the one sure thing that results from Lean Six Sigma initiatives. As has been said, the Project Sponsor will encounter different responses to change. People choose to change, but whether they will or will not change or adapt to change is the onus of a leader, as success required them to change. As I said previously, some people would have jumped to the other side of the fence; some will still be on the fence, while others will be holding back. In addition to differences in reactions, the Sponsor also has to deal with the fact that people adjust to change at different rates. Because change is inevitable and resistance unavoidable, the Sponsor has no choice but to deal with it, purposely and effectively.

The concept of change in the context of a HOW in sponsoring is the Sponsor acting as a change manager, and in a more specific sense, following the change management plan to achieve clarity, criticality, commitment and consistency.

I propose John Kotter's 8-step model for driving change as a change management roadmap for the Sponsor.

Eight-Step Change Management

| Step | Action |
|------|--------|
| 1 | Create a sense of urgency |
| 2 | Build a powerful guiding coalition |
| 3 | Get the vision right |
| 4 | Communicate for buy-in |
| 5 | Empower action and remove obstacles |
| 6 | Create short-term wins |
| 7 | Build the changes |
| 8 | Anchor the changes in corporate culture for sustainability |

*Figure 5.1 – Kotter's Eight-Step Change Management Model*

## Step 1 – Create a sense of urgency

According to Kotter, the first and most crucial step to managing change is to build a sense of urgency. This has been sufficiently discussed in *Chapter 3*. It is important to get the whole organisation inspired to want to change and then maintain this momentum throughout the project. However, it should be stressed that this sense of urgency should not be panic-driven, borne out of fear of losing jobs, for example. The urgency should focus on the external and should stress risks and opportunities that can bolster market position, for example. Although internal metrics should not be ignored, a Sponsor should give more attention to external metrics.

Here are some ways in which you could drive urgency:

- Conduct SWOT analysis, scenario planning and a wide range of strategic planning tools

- Conduct extensive dialogues with stakeholders and process owners

- Formulate results and communicate the business case dramatically, stressing on the problem, the consequences if ignored, and the benefits if addressed

- Make justification why a proposed change should be prioritised

It is the role of the Sponsor to keep the initiative top-of-mind for the key stakeholders. Through simple actions such as including a sentence in weekly email updates, adding the project as a standing agenda item to monthly meetings or just stopping past the desk of key participants for a chat, all help maintain the momentum of the initiative. Furthermore, these actions ensure the Sponsor is better placed to identify threats and opportunities, assess organisational and individual abilities and possible contributions, and draw more people, including customers into the fold. Failure to create a sense of urgency is starting on the wrong foot. However, starting on a false sense of urgency is equally, if not, more disastrous.

## Step 2 – Build a powerful guiding coalition

Sponsors should start creating the momentum for change by convincing influential individuals within the organisation to join a guiding coalition. By harnessing the team-building and emotional commitment of true leaders across all rungs and divisions of the organisation the Sponsor's change efforts will have the greatest impact.

A practical way to start building the support coalition is to identify possible key influencers, analyse the extent of their influence and determine ways to maximise their potential. You should also include in your inventory those you deem are disablers or negative influencers because you also need to address their issues. As much as possible, you want as many stakeholders to be on the bus because if they are with you, they may sit in the front row. It is better for the project team if they are on the bus rather than out of the bus. You can use the chart below to build your inventory.

| Names | Title/Position | Power | Expertise | Network | Tasks |
|---|---|---|---|---|---|
| Trailblazers | | | | | |
| 1 | | | | | |
| 2 | | | | | |
| ... | | | | | |
| Advocates | | | | | |
| 1 | | | | | |
| 2 | | | | | |
| ... | | | | | |
| Uncertain | | | | | |
| 1 | | | | | |
| 2 | | | | | |
| ... | | | | | |
| Passive Resisters | | | | | |
| 1 | | | | | |
| 2 | | | | | |
| ... | | | | | |
| Active Opponents | | | | | |
| 1 | | | | | |
| 2 | | | | | |
| ... | | | | | |

## Step 3 – Get the vision right

The third step is to unify thinking into one powerful vision in the organisation. The vision will help people understand what a particular project aims to achieve, why there is a need to work together and what is expected of them.

This is aggressively driving clarity and criticality about the Lean Six Sigma vision. The vision speech should be short, succinct and powerful. It is easier to spread the vision if it is two sentences long. A long and complicated vision story is in danger of being misunderstood, forgotten, trivialised, or ignored.

## Step 4 – Communicate for buy-in

The fourth step then requires the Sponsor to communicate the vision to as many people as possible and make the vision "shine" among other organisational objectives. Keeping the vision fresh and appealing every day makes it more memorable. Most importantly, the change manager should lead by example. To "walk-the-talk" is the most powerful communication medium available to a Sponsor.

You should go back to the inventory you created in Step 2 and expand the list to include other people who should be engaged in the improvement process.

## Step 5 – Empower action and remove obstacles

Sponsors also need to identify and remove obstacles to make it easier for the project team to implement their project and for the rest of the organisation to adapt to the new working environment. The change manager should engage the help of other change leaders within the business and not feel like they have to remove all the obstacles themselves. That is why they created a guiding coalition at the start of the project.

A worksheet for managing barriers and obstacles could look like this:

| Type/Source of Obstacles and Barriers | Solutions | Timeframe | Persons Responsible |
|---|---|---|---|
| Government (Legislative and Regulatory) | | | |
| 1 | 1 | | |
| 2 | 2 | | |
| ... | ... | | |

| Organisational Level | | | |
|---|---|---|---|
| 1 | 1 | | |
| 2 | 2 | | |
| ... | ... | | |
| Local Level | | | |
| 1 | 1 | | |
| 2 | 2 | | |
| ... | ... | | |
| Resources | | | |
| 1 | 1 | | |
| 2 | 2 | | |
| ... | ... | | |
| Project Team | | | |
| 1 | 1 | | |
| 2 | 2 | | |
| ... | ... | | |
| Others | | | |
| 1 | 1 | | |
| 2 | 2 | | |
| ... | ... | | |

You may add some more rows and columns as you see fit. It becomes more useful if you are able to capture all the possible roadblocks that your team may encounter.

## Step 6 – Create short-term wins

Before the project ends, a change manager should identify short-term wins and recognise efforts in interim victories, even if they appear small. This will motivate people to aspire to achieve more successes and will also act as a counterbalance to nay-sayers. To support their change effort and make it easier for short-term wins to happen, the Sponsor should create short-term, sure-fire targets that are easily achieved without much effort and investment.

Short-term wins should be:

**VISIBLE** – "It is real and not just hype!"

**UNAMBIGUOUS** – "This is where we were. This is where we are now!"

**LINKED TO LEAN SIX SIGMA** – "Lean Six Sigma it is and not anything else!"

However, when celebrating short-term wins, it is important not to declare the project as a whole a success too early – remember, real and meaningful change is only achieved in the long term.

## Step 7 – Build the changes

Step seven is all about the Sponsor making change continuous, sustaining the project's momentum and improving the business' knowledge and skills. For projects that take more than six months to complete, it is a good idea to review the communication and change plan with someone external to the team as a sanity check. This step addresses the consistency and commitment elements of your improvement efforts.

## Step 8 – Anchor the changes in corporate culture for sustainability

The final step requires the change manager to ensure the changes stick and become part of the corporate culture. One of the best examples I have seen of this was a technical director at a global industrials company who continually reiterated the reasons why a large change program succeeded. In his messages, he admitted there were some things that weren't perfect, but for the past three years this manager has used the project successes as a way of keeping the changes at the forefront of operations, ensuring the new processes have become embedded into day-to-day business.

As changes need to be seen and heard at every organisational level and in day-to-day work, repetitive success stories are a good way to make people appreciate the change process. The sustainability of improvements should be supported through conversations that extend to every appropriate role within the business

### Chef Analogy for Change:

When a chef wants to test whether her new recipe is as good as she imagined it to be, she needs to use three things: a recipe (framework), kitchen utensils (tools) and cooking methods (techniques). Without a good recipe, the utensils and cooking methods are useless. Without the proper kitchen utensils, cooking methods and recipes are also worthless. If the techniques are mediocre, the chef could not produce a good dish even if the framework is in place and the best cooking gadgets are available. The chef has to make sure that when cooking, the recipe should be followed using the right utensils and skilfully applying the techniques at the right time.

## 3. Coaching

*"You do not lead by hitting people over the head — that's assault, not leadership." – Dwight D. Eisenhower (34th President of the United States)*

Leaders need to use human nature to assist in accomplishing their visions. A coaching strategy allows the leader to create gentle ripples to influence others to embrace change, rather than resist, through directive style. Coaching also allows the project leader to grow through developing their thinking rather than as a result of the Sponsor just giving them the answer.

Most organisations and Sponsors talk about coaching their team, but as soon as the project is on the critical path, the Sponsor shirks away from a coaching role, straight past mentor and into a directive role. Sometimes coaching is seen merely as a passive skill, only applied when the project manager comes to the Sponsor with a problem. Experience has shown that the coaching element is easily rectified when the Sponsor does not abdicate responsibility of the project. I have seen many instances where the Sponsors are very busy people. They delegate the project to a trained project manager and contact the project leader only when things are already going wrong which is always too late.

I have found that as soon as I introduce the Sponsor to the Chef/ Restaurant Analogy, and tell them that their reputation is still on the line, they realise the need to guide the project leader by asking a few pertinent questions (see *Chapter 2* on the art of questioning and *Appendix 1* on tollgate questions for more detailed and specific questions; strategic and objective coaching for getting people out of the drama of the situation are provided in *Appendix 2*). When I see Sponsors shift to the directing mode, I usually ask only one or maybe two questions – how does the project leader feel when you dictate to them what to do, and how empowered do they feel, or how can you as their Sponsor help them learn for themselves from this situation?

Coaching is an effective tool to enhance productivity and performance yet, all too often, Sponsors mistake coaching for mentoring. The coach gets the coachee to do the thinking and learning themselves, whereas the mentor shares their knowledge and experience with the mentee and advises them on the path forward. Despite the best intentions, Sponsors who assume the role of mentor try to advise the project leader what to do and how to do it and inadvertently run the project. My advice to these Sponsors has been to understand when they need to be a mentor and offer advice, and when to sit back, ask the coaching question and let the project leader do some reflection and learning, before guiding them. This is the challenge and where the ability to ask questions really comes in (see section on the art of questioning in *Chapter 2*). Tollgate or milestone checklists (see checklist in *Appendix 1*) are also a good source of coaching questions.

Coaching does not mean imposing of one's vision but rather it is about facilitating opportunities for the team members to accept and embrace your vision as a Project Sponsor. As a result of coaching, the team will be focused on the goal and perform at their best through their own initiative. Even with the best of intentions, sponsoring efforts fail when effective coaching is not applied. The Sponsor should be able to not only coach the team to support the vision of the Lean Six Sigma project but should extend efforts to assist them in performing shifting roles and responsibilities within the context of organisational changes.

There are several coaching models that a Project Sponsor could adapt. However, the basic principles of an effective coaching strategy are:

- Conviction-driven

- Dynamic and participative process

- Based on honesty, trust and integrity

- Anchored on the ability to understand people and their personal needs and motivations

- Focused on commitment to action and the development of new ideas

- Demands impartiality and ignores prejudice

- Requires mental and emotional fitness

- Amount of coaching depends on individual needs and characteristics

- Relies on skilled questioning and listening with empathy

According to Keith Rosen in his book, *Coaching Salespeople Into Sales Sponsors*, a coaching edge allows the manager to give his people the "tough, edgy support often required to propel people to the next level of success while being mutually supportive and empowering", and without tarnishing his or her pure intentions, and maintaining commitment of the workers.

Here are some examples of questions illustrating how the coaching edge may be used:

- Can I point something out to you that may be tough for you to look at right now?

- Can I share with you what I see and then we can work this out together?

- There's something that I see that may be uncomfortable to hear, and I just want to make sure that you are ready to hear it. Is it okay if I move forward in discussing this with you?

- Do I have permission to say something to you each time I notice that you are reverting to your old destructive habits or behaviours?

- Can I push you a little harder to develop a better way to manage your schedule that will more than double your productivity each day?

- I want you to know that whatever we discuss right now will be held in the strictest of confidence. I refuse to compromise my integrity, and my word. I want this meeting to be a safe place for you to feel comfortable sharing with me how you're feeling and what you see as the real issue that needs to be addressed. This way I can best support you in overcoming it/creating the right solution for you. How does that sound?

According to Ken Blanchard, renowned management and leadership guru, there are four stages of leadership coaching and participation:

1. Directing – The coach instructs individuals who lack knowledge on new competencies required (e.g. technical, advanced statistical, leadership, team-building, and people skills) until such time that the member gains new insights, a sufficient understanding of the requirements of the job and a new appreciation of their experiences. This is a mentor not a coaching role, e.g. go see this person, do this/ do that etc.

2. Coaching – The team member could already independently perform his functions with minimal assistance. The coach intervenes only when there is a problem to be resolved such as when a project goal is not met.

3. Delegating – After sufficient training and coaching, the member masters the required skills, competently performs his functions

without assistance and displays desired behaviours. The coach delegates full responsibility.

4. Supporting – The coach is relegated to a scaffolding role. He or she continues to drive peak performance by encouragement and recognition of accomplishments.

Practically, this means a Project Sponsor should:

- Make an inventory of the knowledge, skills and talents at the individual and team level and their needs and motivations

- Diagnose strengths and weaknesses of the team members; identify opportunities for improvements vis-à-vis project goals and performance standards

- Identify points of resistance to change; establish reasonable hange goals within the context of the project

- Craft a coaching strategy to enhance influence and coaching effectiveness which incorporates a recognition and reward system and evaluation criteria

- Review responsibilities, action steps and confirm commitment from team members

- Delegate new roles and responsibilities and provide scaffolding to develop competence

When the Sponsor sees that the project team or one of its members are going wayward, it is a good decision for the Sponsor to wear his or her coaching hat. Although some organisations hire the services of an external coach, it does not mean that the Sponsor should shirk away from that important role of coaching when his or her intervention is most opportune. Being the team's Sponsor, he or she is in a vantage position to sense when problems arise and to know whether or not individual members and the team as a whole have the knowledge and skills to deal with the challenges.

Coaching is not limited to the development of knowledge and skills to enhance individual and team performance. Coaching is also about guiding the team when their commitment wavers or when their efforts become inconsistent. Through a coaching strategy skilfully used, the Sponsor is able to lead individuals to look into their strengths and capabilities, and tap their energy and talents to solve problems on their own. In this sense, coaching has that unique capability to induce workers to honour their commitment thereby ascribing accountability to themselves.

Coaching may also be used to clarify issues and problems. Sponsors should remember that improvement projects are often most vulnerable after the initial phase when effects (or the turbulence) of change efforts start to peak. Coaching skills come to play to guide the team to rethink and refocus. However, the Sponsor should not go to the extent of solving a problem for the team. He or she should let them discover how to solve it, otherwise they will become completely dependent on the Sponsor.

### Chef Analogy for Coaching:

The kitchen is literally and figuratively the hottest place in restaurant. When pressure builds or tensions arise due to some glitches, kitchen workers can sometimes be seen screaming and mouthing bad language. The executive chef can use her coaching edge to restore order in the kitchen.

## 4. Communication

> *"The art of communication is the language of leadership." – James Humes*
> *(Lawyer, author and presidential speechwriter)*

Essential to the success of all the other seven Cs is communication. An effective communication system enables the Project Sponsor to exert influence upwards and downwards in the organisation. Miscommunication or lack of communication causes conflict, confusion, paranoia and distrust. Neglecting the potential of a good communication strategy hampers the Sponsor's opportunities to bolster clarity of the Lean Six Sigma project imperatives, dampens commitment of stakeholders and team members, projects inconsistency, and compromises change management efforts. Good communication skills also help the Sponsor to perform his or her roles as an effective coach and enabler. A well written charter is a powerful communication tool as it is.

The Sponsor's role in the communications area is to be like a mean ruthless editor of a newspaper. Key to communication is: it's better being blunt than bland!

I wish to reiterate here that in communicating to stakeholders, the Sponsor should remember that to gain buy-in, a COMPLEX business situation or problem should be made SIMPLE which makes it COMPELLING. For the message to get through to the intended recipient, the language should be clear and simple, the tenor should be urgent, and the delivery accurate and timely.

Communication is a powerful tool that the Sponsor should use to demonstrate the urgency of the project and to gain support from all concerned. Visible sponsoring demonstrates management's commitment to change and this radiates through to the bottom line. Such commitment can only be brought out through a properly implemented communication plan with compelling messages about:

- The need for change

- The requirements of change

- The benefits of change

- The negative outcomes if change does not happen

Barriers to the success of Lean Six Sigma projects can only be minimised by creating open relationships, which means the Project Sponsor has to reach out and create such relationships. Openness and consistency in all forms of communication are the cornerstone of a good communication system.

Constant communication also helps breed a common language especially among the Lean Six Sigma team, drives change and creates a Lean Six Sigma culture. The Project Sponsor should ensure that the right message is conveyed to the right people and at the right time. Especially during the deployment stage, questions about the nature, benefits and criticality of the Lean Six Sigma approach should be communicated in a clear, concise and systematic manner.

Pertinent facts should be communicated. When both project strengths and weaknesses are properly communicated to the team, it helps the Project Sponsor to leverage wins, identify difficulties and focus efforts to solve problems. A Sponsor can achieve this by:

- Developing a communication plan anchored on openness and constancy

- Continuously updating and refining the message and the delivery system to clarify the WHATs, WHOs, WHYs, WHENs and HOWs of the Lean Six Sigma project

- Applying a variety of communication media and aids

- Communicating wins to the project team to enhance appreciation and instil motivation to success

- Communicating project failures and difficulties to allow for improvement

- Keeping communication lines open and encourage feedback

Initially, the Sponsor may devise a very simple communication plan such as the following:

| Objective | Audience/Target | Strategy | By Whom | By When |
|-----------|-----------------|----------|---------|---------|
|           |                 |          |         |         |

Later on as the DMAIC project progresses and as more details come into the picture, the Sponsor may formulate a more comprehensive communication strategy that should contain the following:

I.  Key Messages

- Description of key message or information to be communicated

- Examples of key messages are:

  - project imperatives
  - benefits of the Lean Six Sigma initiative, both tangible and intangible
  - schedule of activities
  - updates
  - progress reports
  - problem consultation
  - changes

II.  Objectives

- Why are you sending these messages?

III.  Target Audience and Recipients

- Indicate names, designations, and addresses if need be

- Specify groups or organisational units

IV.  Communication Channels and Strategies

- Choose the most effective medium of communication

- Communication may be verbal or non-verbal

- Channels may include the following:

    - paper documents
    - e-mail
    - electronic documents
    - videos
    - seminars and workshops
    - intranet/internet, webcasts
    - bulletin boards
    - company newsletters, briefings
    - announcements, handouts
    - press releases
    - face to face meetings

V.  Persons Responsible

- Assign who should relay key messages and who should retrieve feedback and information from the recipients

- Can be an individual, a group or team who are most capable of delivering the message in a timely and accurate manner

VI.  Schedule and Timeframe

- Indicate delivery frequency (weekly, monthly, etc.)

- Schedule two-way communication

- Specify when the message should be delivered and timeframe when feedback is due

VII. Feedback Mechanism

- Describe feedback log, indicate the process for handling feedback

- Describe how objections will be identified and handled

- Describe how to manage negative publicity

VIII. Referrals
- Reference then communicate activity to any supporting project, organisational unit or business process/operation taking place as part of the project

IX. Comments and Recommendations
- Include here resulting problems or issues

- Write observations that do not fall under any of the above headings

- Include recommendations if any

At this juncture, I would like to emphasise that communication is not simply making information available or passing on messages. Communication is a two-way street. For communication to be productive, a Sponsor must have good communication skills. I will not delve on the details of what constitute good communication skills but I will venture on some quick tips to improve one's communication skills in the lens of change management.

1. Communication is both verbal and non-verbal. Duck (1999) in the Harvard Business Review said, "Everything managers say – or don't say – delivers a message." People will most likely give more meaning to your behaviour. The cliché is true – actions speak louder. Eloquence is drowned when people sense you do not mean what you are saying.

2. A message is as credible as the highest credible source that will communicate it. Communication should be anchored on honesty, openness, competence, commitment and empathy. Without these, you will not gain the trust of the people around you.

3. Emphasise what matters to the person you are talking to. Resistance to a change is reduced when it is presented with a definable level of benefit.

4. When unnecessary, avoid being too technical to people. Put yourself in their shoes and talk to each of them in their own language.

5. Communicate performance and successes. It lets people know they are involved, boosts their sense of pride, and enhances their level of commitment.

6. Don't forget the negatives. If you don't tell people the bad news, someone else will. Better that you do it and make sure that the information is accurate.

7. Communication is also about listening. Good listening skills build trust and respect. Always institute feedback mechanisms to give your people the opportunity to vent their opinions and concerns.

8. As long as the circumstances allow, it is more rewarding to communicate in person.

9. Reinforce messages by communicating early and often. Get people into the loop.

10. Do not forget the purpose of communicating. Do not go around the bush or you will lose the message and also your credibility.

A number of change management experts consider communication the key ingredient of an effective change management strategy. In the people perspective of change, Hersey and Blanchard argued,

> *"Good communications are the lifeblood of any enterprise, large or small, communications are essential to keep our entire organization functioning at maximum levels and to make the most of our greatest management resource – our people."*

## Chef Analogy for Communication:

There are many people who work underneath the chef, each one assigned a specific task. At peak hours, the kitchen atmosphere borders on intense to explosive. A chef with good communication skills is able to communicate her requirements well to her people amidst all the noise. The chef has to have a strong voice to dish out orders and also to coordinate the frenzied activities so as not to compromise the quality of the dishes and to ensure timely delivery to the customer's table.

# 6

# Applying the 8 Cs Framework

The level of competence of a Project Sponsor makes or breaks a Lean Six Sigma project. They perform the gruelling role of negotiating through the tricky and difficult path towards project success. They make things and people work together like a well-oiled machine. Since Lean Six Sigma is essentially an organisational initiative or an initiative anchored on team or group effort, it is useful to take a pragmatic approach to sponsoring change. The 8 Cs framework (Clarity, Criticality, Change, Commitment, Consistency, Charter, Coaching and Communication) provides a structured approach to performing one's role as a Project Sponsor all throughout the Six Sigma initiative and beyond, and to solving problems and distilling threats to success.

Despite the best laid plans, any Lean Six Sigma project is bound to encounter challenges in progress, acceptance, and commitment to the project etc. along the way. The following are some of the common problems encountered in Lean Six Sigma initiatives from my experience:

1. Project charters that are too vague, change too often or suffer from scope creep.

2. Team members who do not all share one unified direction.

3. Team leaders or members who are not the right fit (e.g. wrong skill set or functional representation).

4. Team members or leaders who are not working fast enough, do not spend sufficient time on projects or become bogged down by analysis paralysis.

5. Frustration and discouragement of some improvement teams, brought on by pressure for immediate financial impact.

6. Key stakeholders who are not fully supportive of the team's methods or solutions (either by not cooperating or by undermining them).

7. Improvement team solutions that are unworkable, insufficient, not innovative enough, or too radical.

8. Inadequate budget to complete project or implement recommended solutions.

9. Competing and/or conflicting project objectives among different teams (lack of integration).

10. Competing demands on Sponsor's time from multiple projects.

With these common problems in mind, it is important for the Sponsor to understand some key myths and pitfalls to avoid in the project rollout (list based on Cygi, et al.):

1. **Not allowing enough time** – Lean Six Sigma initiatives take time. Organisational speed and momentum will wane. Therefore time and effort of team members should be dedicated to the completion of the project. The allocation of time should include enough time for people to go through and accept the change.

2. **Lack of an identified leader** – Individual independent efforts are not enough. A project leader should be designated to provide direction and progress (see roles detailed in Chapter 1).

3. **Taking too big a bite** – The scope of the project is too broad resulting in lack of focus. If the project scope is too large then the team feels it is unachievable because it will take years or just seems impossible.

4. ***Focusing on isolated pockets*** – This is caused by the failure to institute a uniform and pervasive campaign in the entire organisation.

5. ***"But we're different"*** mentality – The organisation or the team believes that it is so unique that it refuses to believe that what's worked for others could possibly work for them.

6. ***Overtraining*** – Not all Six Sigma tools have to be used in one project. This is where you need the Master Black Belt to be pragmatic and use only the tools required to identify root causes and not use tools for the sake of use or academic rigour.

7. ***Blindly believing your measurement system*** – This is caused by the failure to validate measurements. Sometimes errors are introduced during data collection that will identify incorrect root causes or exaggerate the contribution of that root cause to the problem.

The 8 Cs framework could be used to address these problems and to avoid falling into common pitfalls. Here are just some of the ways of applying the 8 Cs framework. The proposed solutions are not exhaustive.

*Project Pitfall 1:* **Vagueness, broadness (or diminutiveness), uncertainty of project scope**

| | |
|---|---|
| **Clarity** | Make a clear connection between activities and project goals and ultimately the overall organisational vision. The project should be communicated to and well understood by the team members. |
| **Criticality** | Ensure that the project scope addresses CTQs and set realistic expectations. The project objective should be urgent and critical to organisational business. |
| **Charter** | Ensure that the charter is well-defined and focused. It should explain what the team is expected to accomplish and what is out of scope of the project. It should include milestones/deliverables and timelines. It should specify the process and process boundaries. |

## Project Pitfall 2: **Lack of unified direction/weak leadership**

| | |
|---|---|
| Clarity | Specify individual roles and responsibilities and the working relationships of individuals and sub-working groups. |
| Commitment | Ensure that activities are under control and keeping in phase with prior demands in the matter of productivity. |
| Charter | Establish or revise the objectives and activities with the participation of the team members responsible in achieving them. |
| Change | Leverage the change coalition to exemplify the behavioural requirements of the changes that the Lean Six Sigma entails. |
| Coaching | Administer a detailed deployment plan that includes, among others: 1) specific responsibilities of team members, stakeholders and management, 2) project proposals, 3) project review agendas and tracking, and 4) impact of the Lean Six Sigma initiative. |
| Clarity | Ensure documentation of the Lean Six Sigma process to resolve any confusion and to control the direction of activities and processes. |
| Communication | Emphasise the need for cooperation and strong leadership, build synergy through proper communication channels and media. |

## Project Pitfall 3: **Wrong fit of team members, overtraining**

| | |
|---|---|
| Commitment | Secure the involvement of individuals from various organisational units to ensure functional representation. |
| Charter | Include in the charter the required knowledge and skill sets as well as training needs. |
| Change | Ensure that the right people are selected as team members. The rule is – impart the right knowledge to the right person at the right time. |
| Coaching | Ensure team members, senior executive team, and deployment sponsors are trained only on the tools and techniques needed to push the project. Do not waste time and effort on unnecessary training. |

## Project Pitfall 4: **Lack of time and commitment**

| | |
|---|---|
| Commitment | Motivate team members to optimise productivity through compensation, rewards, recognition and promotion through visible leadership as the Sponsor. |
| Criticality | Ensure that project leaders dedicate their time and energy to the Lean Six Sigma project so as not to be bogged down by other organisational duties. Lean Six Sigma initiatives require deliberate focus. If necessary talk to the project manager or team member's direct manager to gain commitment of their time to deliver the project. |
| Coaching | Encourage timeliness and resolve analysis paralysis through regular progress reviews, constant communication and feedback. The Project Sponsor should initiate dialogues to determine problems and issues that affect performance. |
| Communication | Set up dialogues with your team to thresh out sources of problems and agree on solutions. |

## Project Pitfall 5: **Failure to address resistance to change, anxiety and discouragement**

| | |
|---|---|
| Clarity | State the imperatives of change in simple and understandable terms. Emphasise how employees would benefit from change. |
| Commitment | Celebrate successes and recognise individual and team achievements. |
| Criticality | Establish a change management plan that highlights the need for supportive behaviours and skills, and that elucidates the urgency of the change initiative. |
| Change | Develop good HR strategies to build a happy culture. Be the happy face of change; lead the change. |
| Coaching | Avoid creating a blame culture by creating a shared risk and reward system. Show energy and enthusiasm in supporting the Six Sigma initiative. |
| Communication | Formulate and implement a communication plan that spans vertically and horizontally throughout the organisation. Communicate quick wins to dispel discouragement and to sustain momentum. |

*Project Pitfall 6:* **Lack of support from management**

| Criticality | Identify bottlenecks and constraints stemming from the top and seek help of the change coalition to address these problems. |
|---|---|
| Change | Convince executive leadership and peers of the auspiciousness of the Lean Six Sigma initiative. Explain the alignment between the Lean Six Sigma project and overall organisational objectives. |
| Coaching | Quickly find solutions to inadequate budget and resources. Support and advocate for those who demonstrate leadership across lateral boundaries. |
| Communication | Ensure senior level commitment to the Lean Six Sigma initiative and communicate their support throughout the organisation. Educate business executives, partners and peers on how the work pipeline converts into profit. |

*Project Pitfall 7:* **Lack of integration**

| Change | Integrate Lean Six Sigma into the core of the organisational strategy and vision, and continuously communicate progress reports to top management. Use authority and influence to solve cross-functional problems and use the change coalition as a means to destroy barriers and to nurture synergy and cooperation. |
|---|---|
| Consistency | Identify and address competing or conflicting project objectives. Align project activities to overall organisational strategy and discard activities that are distractive or that are not consistent to the overall objective. |

I have shown how the 8 Cs framework could be applied in specific situations where the Lean Six Sigma project finds difficulty. The recommended ways are not comprehensive. It's up to the Sponsor to put together a hybrid approach following the basic principles of each C and by reaching intuitively into personal experience.

Regardless of the approach you take, you as a Project Sponsor should be tough on your decisions, confronting people and situations without let-up. Sure, some people will get angry at you. Some people will get upset. But when you make the right decision from among a range of difficult choices, success is sure to follow. And in success, you redeem their trust and the creative people behind the success will doff their hats to you and respect you more.

Making the right (and honourable) decisions and avoiding the wrong turns is a skill derived from intuitive experience. A Sponsor enriches his or her experience by honing sponsoring skills. How you may do this is explained in the next chapter.

# 7

# Continuing to Improve
# Your Sponsor Skills

By now, you realise that being a skilful Sponsor is challenging in many ways. As the Sponsor of change, you become its face, you become its catalyst. Too easy to say, but tricky. You need to have the knowledge and skills, the charisma, the resilience, the commitment to be an effective catalyst of change. We have learnt the values, the skills and tools that should be stashed in your cache. You have to use them, and use them well, to sharpen these skills. Other readily available and effective mechanisms to sharpen your Sponsor skills are through feedback and formal assessment.

## *Feedback Mechanisms*

For Lean Six Sigma Sponsors giving and receiving feedback is a key to the success of improvement initiatives. It indicates the Sponsor's willingness to accept accountability, to learn new ways of doing things or to look at things in a different way. An effective feedback mechanism allows organisational members, regardless of rank or function, to understand how they are affected by the change initiative and how they could contribute to the success of the Lean Six Sigma project. For this to happen, it is important that the feedback loop goes up and down the organisation, involving team members, functional representatives, peers and lateral partners, executive leadership, process owners and other stakeholders.

The feedback process is a communicative tool that allows Project Sponsors to advocate Lean Six Sigma and visibly demonstrate their commitment to the initiative. Aside from formal tollgate reviews and progress reports, Project Sponsors should also hold private or closed-door dialogues and consultations with team members, peers, and organisational leaders and executives to better understand the problems and needs of project team members.

In preparing for feedback, it would be worthwhile to consider the following areas:

- Written – active versus passive
- Oral – speaking and listening
- Visual – learning maps
- Internally and externally focused
- Formal (reports) and informal (ad hoc conversations)
- Presentation techniques – visuals and body language
- Meeting management techniques
- Vertical and horizontal directions

Feedback mechanisms also help establish uniform performance standards and unified direction of activities. The following are key points to remember when instituting feedback mechanisms:

1. Focus on key process indicators to diagnose early warning signs of problems and constraints and to give ample time for corrective action.
2. Use structured metrics and dashboards.
3. Ensure clear, complete and simple messages.

4.  Use a variety of media; combine written and oral, formal and informal modes of communication.

5.  Ensure open and honest communication.

6.  Use descriptive language that relates objectively to a specific situation, problem, process or issue.

7.  Respond constructively and with empathy.

8.  Observe respect and diplomacy.

9.  Send message and ask for feedback at the right time and to/from the right person.

10. Use facts and data gleaned from feedback information to adjust standards and to sustain momentum.

11. Master good listening skills (e.g. repeating, paraphrasing, questioning, clarifying, re-hashing, knowledgeable previews, gestures).

12. Avoid labels.

13. Avoid a blame culture.

In terms of honing one's skills, the main thing you want to find out from feedback is possible areas of improvement in your sponsoring skills. It gives you a frame of reference regarding your strengths and weaknesses and regarding which sponsoring techniques work and which do not. In this sense, you have to actively seek feedback. Encourage people to throw in feedback whether positive or negative.

I am reminded again of what Colin Powell said in his book, "The day soldiers stop bringing you their problems is the day you have stopped leading them. They have either lost confidence that you can help them or concluded that you do not care. Either case is a failure of leadership."

As a Sponsor, you must utilise and welcome the feedback mechanism as a powerful leadership tool. Encourage your soldiers to approach you and give feedback.

Aside from feedback, you should subject yourself to evaluation. You could gain more valuable insights as to how you can improve as a Sponsor.

# Assessment of Sponsorship

What's measured gets done. Assessment of a Sponsor's performance and effectiveness is a good way for them to become aware of their strengths and weaknesses, and is a means for self-improvement.

Sponsors should be evaluated not only by team members but also by peers, executives and Master Black Belts. One of the pitfalls of Lean Six Sigma leadership is that Sponsors and project leaders assume horizontal connections. Peers and superiors may not necessarily have the same level of Lean Six Sigma expertise and experience as the Sponsor. Failing to engage in feedback and performance assessment by peers and superiors is failing to establish critical connections and support for project success. Peer evaluation and feedback creates a bi-directional support system whereby peers affirm support and commitment and are responsible for checking frequently to see if they are on track.

The following assessment matrix utilises the 8 Cs framework as the criteria for evaluation. It may be slightly modified so that it can be used by peers and top executives in evaluating a Sponsor's effectiveness in the organisation.

### Sponsorship Evaluation Tool

Evaluate sponsoring in your organisation by checking the appropriate column for each criterion. A space is provided under each set of criteria for comments and suggestions. Be guided by the following Likert Scale with 5 being the highest and 1 being the lowest:

5 – Very Good     4 – Good     3 – Fair     2 – Poor     1 – Very Poor

| CRITERIA | 5 VG | 4 G | 3 F | 2 P | 1 VP |
|---|---|---|---|---|---|
| A. TECHNICAL SKILLS | | | | | |
| 1. Demonstrates knowledge on the basic principles, tools and techniques of Six Sigma including deployment tactics and strategies for establishing metrics, selecting projects, and implementing Six Sigma. | | | | | |
| 2. Understands technical aspects of individual functions and responsibilities of one's job and continuously builds knowledge, keeping up-to-date on the technical or procedural aspects of the job. | | | | | |
| 3. Updates technical and procedural Six Sigma knowledge and skills. | | | | | |
| 4. Applies the appropriate tools and strategies in a timely manner. | | | | | |
| Comments: | | | | | |
| | | | | | |
| B. LEADERSHIP/MANAGERIAL SKILLS | | | | | |
| I. Clarity | 5 VG | 4 G | 3 F | 2 P | 1 VP |
| 1. Clearly expresses thoughts and ideas orally or verbally. | | | | | |
| 2. Verifies data and work results to ensure accuracy of information. | | | | | |
| 3. Seeks information from various sources and from individuals of different backgrounds and experiences to improve planning and aid in decision-making. | | | | | |
| 4. Keeps discussions focused on the Six Sigma purposes. | | | | | |
| 5. Shows clear understanding of both organisational and individual perspectives. | | | | | |

| | | | | | |
|---|---|---|---|---|---|
| 6. Ensures that progress reports are kept and that activities and results are documented to ensure clarity, and for future reference. | | | | | |
| 7. Uses reliable tools and systems to keep track of resources, data, time, and project status. | | | | | |
| 8. Shows a clear understanding of duties and responsibilities as a Sponsor. | | | | | |
| 9. Maintains a communication plan to ensure clarity and focus. | | | | | |
| Comments: | | | | | |

| II. Criticality | 5 VG | 4 G | 3 F | 2 P | 1 VP |
|---|---|---|---|---|---|
| 1. Demonstrates clear awareness of the organisational vision and objectives. | | | | | |
| 2. Identifies organisational priorities and establishes project objective with a realistic sense of what is most important, urgent and critical vis-à-vis organisational resources, time and capability. | | | | | |
| 3. Establishes a sense of urgency for the Six Sigma project and for specific strategies and activities. | | | | | |
| 4. Ensures comprehensive information gathering and analysis before making a decision. | | | | | |
| 5. Recognises and leverages organisational opportunities. | | | | | |
| 6. Exhibits advanced and judicious planning. | | | | | |
| 7. Shows awareness of long-term objectives and seeks support and confirmation from top to bottom. | | | | | |
| 8. Leads the team to think critically about organisational processes, challenges opportunities and priorities. | | | | | |

| Comments: | | | | | |
|---|---|---|---|---|---|
| | | | | | |
| **III. Commitment** | 5 VG | 4 G | 3 F | 2 P | 1 VP |
| 1. Shows a passion for improvement and works zealously with the project team. | | | | | |
| 2. Demonstrates willingness to work beyond minimum job requirements and surpass expectations to motivate others to do the same. | | | | | |
| 3. 3. Strikes a good balance between organisational, group and individual needs and welfare. | | | | | |
| 4. Demonstrates willingness to assume responsibility for failures and problems. | | | | | |
| 5. Serves as a model for unceasing enthusiasm and dedication. | | | | | |
| 6. Shows eagerness to accept new responsibilities. | | | | | |
| 7. Ensures that a reward and recognition plan is in place for team successes and individual achievement. | | | | | |
| 8. Models high trust behaviours. | | | | | |
| Comments: | | | | | |
| | | | | | |
| **IV. Consistency** | 5 VG | 4 G | 3 F | 2 P | 1 VP |
| 1. Aligns Six Sigma strategies to the overall organisational vision. | | | | | |
| 2. Fosters collaborative leadership with peers. | | | | | |
| 3. Ensures cross-functional cooperation and integration of Six Sigma initiative in the organisational strategy. | | | | | |

| | 4. Shows dependability and consistency between words and deeds. | | | | | |
|---|---|---|---|---|---|---|
| | 5. Ensures consistent monitoring of team progress. | | | | | |
| | 6. Ensures thoroughness, timeliness and quality of accomplishment of tasks big or small. | | | | | |
| | Comments | | | | | |

| V. Charter | 5 VG | 4 G | 3 F | 2 P | 1 VP |
|---|---|---|---|---|---|
| 1. Ensures thoroughness and clarity of project plan and all its components. | | | | | |
| 2. Engages the participation of all team members and all units and parties involved in the preparation of the project plan. | | | | | |
| 3. Draws on individual and team knowledge, skills and experience in formulating the project charter. | | | | | |
| 4. Fosters ownership of the project. | | | | | |
| 5. Ensures careful estimation of strategic organisational or financial impact. | | | | | |
| 6. Establishes a systematic roadmap to success. | | | | | |
| 7. Maintains standards and stands firm on the project team to achieve desired outcomes. | | | | | |
| 8. Allows re-planning and modification of the charter. | | | | | |
| Comments: | | | | | |

| VI. Change | 5 VG | 4 G | 3 F | 2 P | 1 VP |
|---|---|---|---|---|---|
| 1. Communicates a compelling vision and need for change through Six Sigma. | | | | | |

| | | 5 VG | 4 G | 3 F | 2 P | 1 VP |
|---|---|---|---|---|---|---|
| 2. | Generates enthusiasm and appreciation across all organisational levels to foster ownership. | | | | | |
| 3. | Enlists the support and commitment of influential organisational members to implement a pervasive campaign to adopt and adapt to the change initiative. | | | | | |
| 4. | Takes the lead in exhibiting model behaviours and attitudes to nurture a common vision for change instead of merely imposing change. | | | | | |
| 5. | Identifies and removes roadblocks, constraints and sources of conflict in the Six Sigma change initiative to unify direction and sustain momentum for change. | | | | | |
| 6. | Shows readiness to try new methods and adapts to change easily and quickly. | | | | | |
| 7. | Obtains the needed resources and implements training plans to implement the change initiative. | | | | | |
| 8. | Evaluates alternatives and varying perspectives to come up with a change management plan acceptable to all parties involved. | | | | | |
| 9. | Builds networks and coalitions within groups and within and outside the organisation to influence others to work towards project success. | | | | | |
| 10. | Recognises successes and celebrates wins to enhance credibility of the change initiative. | | | | | |

Comments:

| VII. Coaching | | 5 VG | 4 G | 3 F | 2 P | 1 VP |
|---|---|---|---|---|---|---|
| 1. | Facilitates the development and honing of skills and knowledge of individual members. | | | | | |
| 2. | Provides clear benchmarks for performance. | | | | | |

| | | | | | |
|---|---|---|---|---|---|
| 3. Maintains a professional, positive and nurturing working relationship with the team. | | | | | |
| 4. Builds teamwork and boosts self-esteem. | | | | | |
| 5. Generates an atmosphere of trust, confidence and solidarity to develop healthy and cooperative working relationships. | | | | | |
| 6. Provides scaffolding and guidance to harness individual and group capability. | | | | | |
| 7. Institutes a feedback mechanism to address complaints and concerns of team members. | | | | | |
| 8. Resolves conflicts through consensus. | | | | | |
| 9. Gives credit where credit is due. | | | | | |
| 10. Distils problem behaviours that impede individual or group performance. | | | | | |
| Comments: | | | | | |

| VIII. Communication | 5 VG | 4 G | 3 F | 2 P | 1 VP |
|---|---|---|---|---|---|
| 1. Implements a comprehensive communication plan that effectively spans the entire organisation vertically and horizontally. | | | | | |
| 2. Keeps team members, lateral partners and top management informed and updated of project status. | | | | | |
| 3. Disseminates useful information on a timely and regular basis. | | | | | |
| 4. Ensures healthy and honest communication, feedback mechanisms and dialogues. | | | | | |
| 5. Shows articulateness and demonstrates good communication and listening skills. | | | | | |
| 6. Utilises a wide variety of communication tools and media. | | | | | |
| 7. Ensures logical and organised flow of meetings and presentations. | | | | | |

Comments:

The assessment system helps the Sponsor clarify expected performance standards and barriers to accomplishment. The information gathered from the assessment will help the Sponsor identify resources and tools needed to improve performance. It helps in drawing the roadmap to professional development.

# 8

# Conclusion

In today's business world, no organisation could afford to stay on a plateau even while it seems its business is already doing very well. Experience shows that big stable companies inevitably meet their downfall because they are eventually overcome by even smaller ones who recognise future needs and market gaps and who never stop planning and improving to meet these needs. Innovation and improvement must be planned and executed well in order to maximise their potential.

Lean Six Sigma projects entail different degrees of change but they always affect three organisational aspects – people, technology and operations. The hardest to manage is the people side of change because human beings are more complicated than technology and processes. Change managers should be able to address systematic (borne out of misunderstanding and lack of skills) and behavioural forms of resistance (derived from feelings and prejudices). Since resistance occurs in all levels of the organisation, Sponsors have to approach change management from an employee's perspective to manage individual change and a manager's perspective to deal with organisational change. The organisational or program level change management should have the following elements: shared change purpose, effective change leadership and powerful engagement processes. The local or individual level should focus on developing commitment of local Sponsors, establishing strong personal connections and sustaining personal performance. Sponsors should remind themselves that a change vision must not be imposed, rather must be embraced and taken as the employee's own because ownership promotes commitment and responsibility.

In order to adjust fully to business change, an organisation must act systematically. As complex as a human body, an organisation must work like a healthy human body with all its parts functioning harmoniously. Peak performance can only be achieved when the physical, mental and spiritual needs are addressed. For an organisation, its processes (physical aspect), policies, plans and procedures (mental aspect), and culture (spiritual aspect) should be vigorously kept in good shape. A glitch in one component affects the performance of other parts of the organisation. A systems perspective is then crucial to ensuring the smooth running of a business organisation like a body hale and hearty.

As change in and around the organisation occurs on a regular basis, improvement initiatives also need to have the speed to change with the times. Only a healthy body can cope up with the required agility and stamina to overcome illness or exhaustion.

Since Lean Six Sigma adopts a systemic approach to organisational improvement, Lean Six Sigma stewards should take to heart the systems perspective in driving change. The mindset of Sponsors of Lean Six Sigma projects should always be geared towards creating the environment for organisational success and not narrowly focusing just on project success. The goals of Lean Six Sigma should then be part of the overarching organisational objective. The DMAIC process which is the basic roadmap of robust Lean Six Sigma projects should be aligned well with long-term organisational vision. As such, Sponsors of Lean Six Sigma projects are expected to go beyond merely being information and data processors. Great Sponsors are boldly creative and pioneering futurists who are able to develop three new things for the Lean Six Sigma project: business context, business relevance and individual meaning. However, the responsibility does not stop here. Successful Sponsors are able to create buy-in for this vision by helping the Lean Six Sigma team to capture it succinctly and package and deliver it clearly and effectively. Sponsors are therefore involved in every phase of improvement projects from planning, to completion and to celebration.

Throughout their stewardship of the improvement process, the Sponsor gets to don several hats depending on the need of a particular situation. Sometimes, they get to wear several hats at the same time.

To iron out conflicts and remove stumbling blocks, Sponsors need to have the skills of a good diplomat. Great Sponsors use diplomatic tact and channels to be able to negotiate for organisational support and pave way for smooth implementation of Lean Six Sigma projects. Sponsors wear the hat of a business expert to be able to integrate their Lean Six Sigma initiatives in the organisation, allocate budget and organisational resources, and provide business guidance and redirection when necessary. Sponsors are themselves visionaries who believe in the power of new ideas and have the charisma to inspire people to cooperate to reach their vision and most often even to go through to unchartered heights. Wearing the hat of a team coach, great Sponsors lead the Lean Six Sigma team to victory by setting performance standards and project benchmarks, ensuring proper training and sustaining commitment and team spirit. As the team mechanic, great Sponsors should be expert troubleshooters to ensure that the team works like a well-oiled machine. It has also been emphasised that the most decisively crucial responsibility of Sponsors is to be adept in change management. As change managers, great Sponsors apply personal, group and organisational dynamics to steer the project team and eventually the entire organisation to adapt to changes required by a Lean Six Sigma project, to maximise its benefits, and to ensure long-term success.

## The DMAIC process

In summary, DMAIC consists of five incremental processes that proceed chronologically and logically. Project Sponsors are the gatekeepers and as the keyholders, they decide whether or not the Lean Six Sigma team is ready to get on to each succeeding stage by making full use of tollgate reviews. In tollgate reviews, Sponsors make use of milestones checklists and rely on good questioning skills to make sure that all criteria and deliverables have been satisfied. In each stage, Sponsors will be faced with some form of resistance from team and organisational members. Sponsors should decide by using evidence such as data, observations and experiences gained in previous stages. Before proceeding with the DMAIC process, Sponsors should assess the four elements of Lean Six Sigma: scale, magnitude, duration, and strategic value. Sponsors should determine the segment of the company that is affected by a proposed change initiative (scale), gauge the extent of modifications to the current situation (magnitude), ascertain the length of the project (duration), and establish its significant outcomes (strategic value).

In the **DEFINE** stage, the team defines the problem, the process and the project outcomes. Sponsors should help the team identify what's really important, determine what's going wrong and how it is affecting stakeholders. It is in this stage that members resist the very idea of change and thus the idea of the project itself is met with cynicism or some form of resistance. Thus, Sponsors should be able to create a mindshare among the team members and emphasise the urgency of the project.

In the **MEASURE** stage, the team collects data on current process performance. Sponsors should help the team situate where the current process is and how well or how badly the organisation is doing. The most common form of resistance in this stage is that members or even organisational leaders are unconvinced that a problem could be unravelled. Sponsors should lead the group to continue data collection and assure them that there is a solution.

In the **ANALYSE** stage, the team analyses data to determine the causes and effects of the identified problem. Sponsors should ensure that the team adheres to Six Sigma principles to properly identify root causes rather than symptoms. Sponsors should be wary of the team being waylaid by "analysis paralysis" and should be quick to identify "quick wins".

In the **IMPROVE** stage, solutions are formulated and selected solutions are piloted. The Sponsor should ensure that aside from expected consequences, all unintended consequences and collateral effects up and down stream are dealt with.

In the **CONTROL** stage, the team sets up control mechanisms to guarantee performance and sustainability of the gains. Sponsors should ensure smooth turnover of the improvement project from the team to the process owner. Gains should be verified and performance standards should be kept in check.

The responsibility of the Sponsors is to guide the project team to work like a well-oiled machine throughout the improvement process. Thus, they need to take a pragmatic approach to sponsoring change.

In a simple overview, the toolkit of a great Sponsor has eight fundamental requirements which I called the 8 Cs Framework. There are four cardinal principles that a great Sponsor should adhere to and four strategic tools to use. The four underlying principles (the WHATs) are clarity, criticality, commitment and consistency. The four essential tools (the HOWs) are charter, change, coaching and communication.

## The 4 WHATs

**Clarity** – The first thing that Sponsors should do is to ensure that the goals, components and framework of a Lean Six Sigma project is compellingly clear, otherwise the team will just waste time and resources. When project objectives are vague, Sponsors are not able to sell the urgency of the problem or the idea of a project itself to the organisational leaders, process owners and their project team. A simple rule of thumb for the Sponsor when faced with a vague idea or complicated problem area is to unravel the COMPLEX, make it SIMPLE and then make it COMPELLING. The 11-year-old test (simplifying ideas to the comprehension level of an 11-year-old) is a simple guideline. Clear alignment of project goals to organisational priorities, properly delineated roles and responsibilities, standards and benchmarks succinctly spelt out, would all make a brilliant start of a Lean Six Sigma initiative.

**Criticality** – Criticality simply implies choosing which battles to fight and to wage NOW. It is driving a sense of urgency, instilling a compulsive determination to stakeholders so that the project is PRIORITISED over others. Sponsors should be mindful of these pivotal questions: Why is this project more important than all the others/my day job? Why do this project right now? What happens if we do nothing? A great Sponsor should highlight what is urgent, why it is urgent, and how to address the urgency.

Using powerful stories (rather than high level presentations) highlighting the urgency stirs up feelings to MOVE NOW, PREVAIL and TRIUMPH. Stories are also uniquely capable of contextualising experiences to inspire organisational members to share one's vision of change.

**Commitment** – Sincerity and steadfastness to the means and ends of a process improvement project builds focus and sustains both personal capability and team effectiveness until project completion. A great Sponsor not only motivates the project team to stay committed but he or she should demonstrate their personal commitment through active involvement in all phases and should show sincere desire to address the individual needs. As said, the members can only trust the Sponsor to the degree to which the Sponsor is committed to individual integrity and well-being. In demonstrating high trust behaviours, embracing accountability, and modelling active enthusiasm, a great Sponsor is able to more effectively promote similar behaviours and instil a lean culture in the organisation.

**Consistency** – The significance of this principle in Lean Six Sigma projects is this: consistency builds trust, trust builds commitment, commitment draws support, support nurtures attitude, attitude bolsters synergy, synergy enhances success. A great Sponsor shows their consistency by demonstrating strict adherence to the principles of Lean Six Sigma from start to finish. He or she shows consistency in both tangible and intangible aspects of the project thereby creating a mould by which the team members more willingly expend their creative energies. There should be consistency between words and deeds. Decisions should be coherent to Lean Six Sigma philosophy. Sponsors should be unremitting in monitoring project details and milestones. By consistently showing up, speaking up, and owning up, Sponsors may find it easier to establish performance standards and expectations and sustain project focus.

Consistency allows Sponsors to gain respect and trust from above and from below. A track record of consistency to Lean Six Sigma projects may very well be the most effective scheme for Sponsors to boost their professional brand and value proposition as a great Sponsor.

## The 4 HOWs

**Charter** – The project charter is a pivotal document that serves as a "bible" of the Lean Six Sigma team. When properly presented, the project charter nurtures a sense of ownership and encourages responsibility and accountability, thus it serves as a binding contract or a conscience document which compels the performance of obligations.

One important guideline in writing project charters is to articulate the problem statement in two simple sentences. In and out of scope should be properly spelt out in order not to clutter the objectives of the project. Roles and responsibilities as well as a project tracking system should be incorporated.

Sponsors should remind themselves as well as their team that the project charter is not set in stone, nor is it a cure-all document. It should be allowed to evolve in light of new discovery or information so as not to unduly lock down the project. Most importantly, the project charter should be communicated to all stakeholders to gain support.

**Change** – Change must be managed and cannot be allowed to happen on its own. Thus, the concept of change in the context of a HOW in sponsoring refers to the Sponsor's change management skills and to the change management plan. An effective management strategy allows the Sponsor to address change on two levels: organisational and individual. The change management plan is the most crucial tool of the Sponsors in order to drive change and integrate it in the corporate culture for long-term sustainability. Integrating the Changefirst Wheel's six critical success factors for change management with that of Kotter's 8-step management approach would give Sponsors a useful guide in preparing a distinctive change management strategy to suit their organisations. As a short summary, the eight steps in managing change are: 1) creation of a sense of urgency, 2) building of a powerful guiding coalition, 3) getting the vision right, 4) communicating for buy-in, 5) empowering action and removing obstacles, 6) creating short-term wins, 7) building the changes, and 8) anchoring the changes in corporate culture. Plans and actions for each step should be anchored on the cardinal WHATs of sponsoring and must utilise the recommended HOWs. Knowledge of individual, group and organisational dynamics is a must for Sponsors.

Most importantly, and because the Sponsors are the role models of the change they wish to inculcate, they must demonstrate willingness and enthusiasm to undergo change themselves. This is the best way to convince the organisation that the proposed change is for the better.

**Coaching** – A good coaching plan allows Sponsors to consciously address the people side of change in a timely and structured manner rather than impulsively as when problems arise or only when difficulties have worsened. Skilful coaching means Sponsors guiding the project team, and not mentoring or directing them. It is not telling them what to do nor doing the work for the members but allowing them to learn. A good coaching plan focuses on enhancing productivity and performance especially in shifting roles and responsibilities within the context of organisational changes. Even when an external coach has been hired by the organisation, Sponsors should still wear their coaching hat especially when their intervention is exigent at the time when turbulent changes or work challenges are at its peak.

**Communication** – Essential to the success of all the other seven Cs is a good communication plan – sending/receiving the right message to/from the right people at the right time. A comprehensive communication strategy enables the Project Sponsor to exert influence upwards and downwards in the organisation. Skilful communication helps in bridging gaps and distilling threats to the success of the project. A proficient communication system built on openness and constancy demonstrates commitment of the senior management and radiates through to the bottom line. Open communication not only gives Sponsors the timely opportunity to send compelling messages but also allows them to be apprised of any issue affecting an improvement project.

Sponsoring change is as tricky as change itself. Change is as complex as the dynamics in modern organisations. As a Sponsor, you are the catalyst of change. You are in the driver's seat. As success is yours, so is failure. The 8 Cs Framework may well come to your aid in devising a strategy to sponsor improvement projects. You may deliberately bolster any one of the Cs to respond to the needs of your team or throw in one or more Cs as you may see fit. Fashion out a hybrid approach following the basic principles of each C and by reaching intuitively into personal experience to suit the dynamics of your respective organisations.

At the end of the day, the Lean Six Sigma Sponsors should find out how well they have done, for this is the only way they may realise whether they are on the right path or whether their sponsoring technique is effective. Two ways of doing this is through feedback and formal evaluation. A feedback mechanism (for example, through progress reports, monitoring reviews, dialogues, consultations and informal meetings) serves to allow organisational members regardless of function or position to share their thoughts, problems and needs and also participate in decision-making. The feedback loop gives Sponsors the opportunity to learn and improve themselves. Submitting themselves to formal evaluation at the end of the project would offer more valuable insights in improving one's sponsoring approach. Evaluation of the Sponsor should be done not only by the project team but also by organisational executives, peers and Belts.

Sponsors should consider themselves as executive chefs whose tour of duty is in the kitchen, the most chaotic part of a dining establishment where the atmosphere borders on hot to explosive. On top of all this frenzy is the experienced chef who deftly manages the kitchen staff to work with speed, precision, enthusiasm and skill and who patiently restores order in the kitchen so that every single diner experiences customer satisfaction whether the Sponsor is in the kitchen or not. The Sponsor works like a skilful chef who needs three basic things: a recipe (framework), kitchen utensils (tools) and cooking methods (techniques). Without a good recipe, the utensils and cooking methods are useless. Without the proper kitchen utensils, the cooking methods and recipes become worthless. Even with the best recipes and utensils, the chef could not come up with a good dish if the cooking technique is tawdry and inept. The chef sees to it that the recipe is followed using the right utensils and the right techniques. Sponsors are like them. In leading improvement projects, they have to anchor their strategy on a feasible approach adroitly managing people even when they are not physically present in the workplace all the time.

Thus far, we can conclude that sponsorship is never too easy, as change has never been. Sponsors in fact should be hard on themselves as they should be tough on their decisions, confronting people and situations without let-up. Making the right decisions will sometimes bring pain on themselves and on their team but when such decisions are the honourable thing to do, successful change is almost always the end result. And in victory, you are sure you will gain respect and establish yourself as a successful Sponsor.

# Milestone Checklist

Milestone checklists could aid the Sponsor in making decisions whether to approve phase closure and the start of the next phase in the DMAIC process.

| DEFINE Milestone | Y | N | Remarks/ Percentage of Completion |
|---|---|---|---|
| A clear project statement agreed upon and communicated | | | |
| A high level process map developed | | | |
| Customers identified and VOC translated into CTQs | | | |
| A project charter developed and approved | | | |
| The project team properly trained | | | |
| MEASURE Milestone | | | |
| Key measures identified | | | |
| Data measurement plan developed and executed | | | |
| Process variation identified and validated | | | |
| Performance capability calculated | | | |
| Process sigma calculated | | | |
| ANALYSE Milestone | | | |
| Potential causes of problem identified | | | |
| Root causes verified by data | | | |
| Improvement goal established | | | |

| | | | |
|---|---|---|---|
| Prioritised list of root causes set and validated | | | |
| **IMPROVE Milestone** | | | |
| Root causes further reduced to vital few high impact factors | | | |
| Proposed solutions developed | | | |
| Solutions pilot-tested | | | |
| Results checked against performance goals | | | |
| Full-scale implementation plan developed incorporating results of pilot-test results | | | |
| **CONTROL Milestone** | | | |
| Procedures of the new method standardised and documented | | | |
| Participants trained in the new method | | | |
| Control plan developed and communicated | | | |
| Monitoring plan approved and communicated | | | |
| Project documentation completed | | | |
| Transfer to process owner completed | | | |
| New learning and knowledge communicated and institutionalised | | | |

# Coaching Questions

## Current Reality Questions

### Vision Questions

Vision questions are focused on what the coachee would like to achieve through the conversation or coaching series. They are the end goals or desired outcomes that provide a focus for the conversation or coaching series. The following questions are derived from the coach training courses of David Rock and Neuro Leadership Group and Dr Rock's books, and adapted over time.

Example questions include:

- What is your objective?

- What is your vision for this area?

- What would you like the desired outcome to be?

- What can you see, feel, hear or sense when you think about the results you would like to achieve in this area?

- Could you paint the picture of the ideal outcome of this issue?

- What do you want to achieve here?

- What is your goal here?

## Thinking Questions

Thinking questions explore the coachee's thinking on the topic being discussed. They are often used to allow the coachee to move into a reflective space and focus on their thinking instead of the problem. They usually lead to an insight or new connection.

Example questions include:

- How long you have you been thinking about this? (days/weeks/ months/years)

- How often do you find yourself thinking this? (How many times each hour/day/week?)

- How frequently are you thinking about it?

- When are you most likely to think about this?

- How long do you think about this for, when you do think about it? (minutes/hours)

- How strong is this thought with you? On a scale from one to ten?

- How important is this topic to you, for example, on a scale of one to ten?

- How high is this in your priorities now, e.g. is it in your top 3, 5 or 10 priorities now?

- What priority would you like it to be?

- How committed are you to resolving this topic, on a scale of one to ten?

- What is the ratio of thinking you do about the problem as compared to the solution?

- How motivated are you to resolve this topic?

- How much effort have you invested in thinking about this?

- How do you feel about the thinking time you have given this so far?

- What common threads do you notice in relation to your thinking about this and other issues? (patterns)

- How clear is your thinking about this?

- What stage are you at in your thinking about this?

- How could you take your thinking to the next step?

- What lens might you be looking through in your thinking?

- What aspects of your thinking are most important/effective?

- How does your thinking about this compare to your thinking about other topics?

- Can you see any gaps in your thinking?

- What needs unpacking?

- What are you not thinking about that might help you find resolution?

- What ideas/thoughts have crossed your mind about this that you may have dismissed?

- How do you feel about what you've done so far?

- From the thinking that you have already done on this, what are the main insights that you have had about this up to now?

- What are your insights so far?

## Reappraisal Questions

Reappraisal questions allow the coachee to look at the situation or issue from another perspective. By stepping outside of their current mind maps/perspective and seeing things from a different angle, they can have insights that can support them to move forward.

Example questions include:

- How could you think about this issue from a different perspective?

- Can you describe this issue as an image or picture?

- Have you ever tried an alternative approach? What were the results?

- If this was your boss dealing with this issue, how do you think they would deal with it? What would they do?

- If this was a personal relationship, how would you handle the issue differently to how you are at work?

- What do you think the other person might be feeling regarding this issue?

- If you could observe this situation from a 3rd person point of view, what do you think you would see?

- How can you look at this issue differently?

- What is a different perspective you could have regarding this issue?

- How might you think differently about this?

- Would you be willing to explore another perspective on this current situation?

- If you could zoom out and look at this issue from afar, what would you notice?

- If this were a friend telling you their story, what would you be saying to them to help them reframe it?

- Imagine you are your future self, 20 years from now, what would you say to your present self?

- If you had a choice, what would you do?

- Let's pretend we are in a theatre and run this situation as a movie. You're sitting in the audience watching the movie, what do you see?

## Labelling Questions

By labelling an emotion, situation, body sensation or experience the coachee is able to dampen down any limbic system response and more effectively use the prefrontal region of their brain. This will mean they can have greater insight into their situation, as they are thinking with greater clarity.

Example questions include:

- If you could label your emotion in one or two words, what would it be?

- Describe in one word how you're feeling in this moment?

- Can you describe in a couple of words the impact this is having on you?

- What are the three key emotions around that?

- Can you label the sensation you're feeling in your body?

- How do you feel when you think about this topic?

- How could you describe what is going on for you in a sentence?

- How would you name your experience, in just a few words?

- If you had to give that a label, what would that be?

- What would be one word or picture that you could associate with this issue regarding your feelings?

- If you look at the impact on others of you being this way, how would you say it in one word?

- How would you describe your team's reaction to you in a short phrase?

- How would you describe your relationship to your subordinates in one word?

- If you were to put a label on this habit, what would that be?

## Mindfulness Questions

Mindfulness questions are focused on the coachee's direct experience in the moment, allowing them to see what is present and discover new insights from what is happening in the moment. This also dampens down the limbic system response and increases the coachee's ability to generate new thinking and insights.

Example questions include:

- What is present for you in this moment?

- Can you describe what is present for you right now?

- Where do you feel about the issue in your body?

- What does this issue feel like? Can you describe the sensations?

- Are you willing to look at what is going on here?

- Are you willing to look deeper into this?

- Is there a theme to what you have discovered?

- Can you describe what you're feeling in your body?

- Can you describe this issue using your different senses, i.e. what do you see, feel, hear, taste, touch and smell?

- Are your beliefs in this area based on facts?

- How are you feeling now compared to when we began this conversation?

- What does your intuition tell you about this situation?

- What is your "gut" feeling about this?

- If you could give me an image of what you are feeling right now, what would it be?

- What's the compelling theme here?

- As you talk about and experience this issue, what are you noticing?

- What feels different now you have said that out loud?

- What is the inner dialogue you have running about this issue?

- What thoughts are going on in the back of your head as you talk about this issue?

- Are there any inner thoughts that you're present to in this moment?

## Explore Alternatives Questions

### Planning Questions

When the vision and new insights have been established, then planning questions will support the coachee to achieve the objective or goal based on their new insights. They explore what the plan or steps are for moving forward.

Example questions include:

- Based on this insight, what do you think would be the next step forward for you?

- What is your plan for achieving these targets?

- Now that you have had this new understanding about the situation, what do you think you can do?

- What planning do we need to implement to ensure your success in this area?

- What are your options, based on this insight?

- Do you have a plan for moving forward in this area?

- How clear is your plan for achieving this objective?

- What are the milestones for achieving this goal?

- What are the major steps for achieving your goal?

## *Target Energy Questions*

### Action Questions

When the vision and planning have been discussed then it is time to explore the specific actions for moving forward. Actions are the tasks that will be completed before the next time the coach and coachee meet to review what has been accomplished.

Example questions include:

- What are you prepared to do to make this goal happen?
- What are some of the alternatives for moving forward in this goal area?
- Do you want to take some action around this?
- Would it be worth doing something about this now?
- What is one step you could take towards that this week?
- How can you apply that insight into other areas of your life now?
- What will you complete by next week?
- How could you apply this new learning?

# Glossary

## Lean Six Sigma Terms

### A

ABC Inventory – A methodology for determining inventory levels based on value, space consumption, and turns.

Activity-Based Costing (ABC) – A costing system that identifies the various activities performed in a firm and uses multiple cost drivers (non-volume as well as the volume based cost drivers) to assign overhead costs (or indirect costs) to products. ABC Costing considers the impact and relationship of cost drivers with activities performed.

Affinity Diagram – A technique for organising individual pieces of information into groups or broader categories.

### B

Bar Chart – A graphical method which depicts how data falls into different categories.

Benchmarking – A comparison tool used to determine the level of process, product, or other successes your company is experiencing when compared to similar companies with similar products or processes, typically competitors.

Bottleneck – The slowest operation (choke point) in a manufacturing process.

Brainstorming – A useful and popular tool that can be used to develop highly creative solutions to a problem.

Breakthrough Improvement – A rate of improvement at or near 70% over baseline performance of the as-is process characteristic.

## C

Capability – It is the maximum achievable results that can be attained in a manufacturing system based on limitations imposed. A comparison of the required operation width of a process or system to its actual performance width. Expressed as a percentage (yield), a defect rate (dpm, dpmo), an index (Cp, Cpk, Pp, Ppk), or as a sigma score (Z).

Cause and Effect Diagram – Also Fishbone Diagram, a diagram shaped like a fishbone which shows all the possible variables affecting a process output measure. The problem/opportunity goes into the head of the fish and there are 6 main bones – the 6Ms – Man, Machine, Measure, Mother Nature, Method, Material.

Change Agent – A person who leads a company from the traditional manufacturing practices and philosophies to becoming a Lean organisation.

Characteristic – A process input or output which can be measured and monitored.

Common Causes of Variation   – Those sources of variability in a process which are truly random, i.e. inherent in the process itself.

Concept Fan – A way of finding different approaches to a problem when all obvious solutions have been rejected. It develops the principle of "taking one step back" to get a broader perspective.

Concurrent Engineering –The reorganisation of product design, development, production planning and procurement processes to take place to the extent possible in parallel (more or less at the same time), utilising multi-disciplinary project teams, electronic information management, and improved communications.

Conflict Resolution Diagram – A tool used to resolve hidden conflicts that usually perpetuate chronic problems.

Control Chart – The most powerful tool of Statistical Process Control. It consists of a Run Chart, together with statistically determined Upper and Lower Control Limits and a Centre Line.

Control Limits – Upper and lower bounds in a Control Chart that are determined by the process itself. They can be used to detect Special or Common Causes of variation. They are usually set at Â±3 Standard Deviations from the central tendency.

Cost of Poor Quality (COPQ) – The costs associated with any activity that is not doing the right thing right the first time. It is the financial qualification of any waste that is not integral to the product or service.

Creative Problem Solving – Methods that combine defining of problems, identification of patterns, generation of new ideas, and action planning to resolve problems with unique and innovative solutions.

Critical to Quality (CTQ) – Any characteristic that is critical to the perceived quality of the product, process or system. See Significant Y.

Critical X – An input to a process or system that exerts a significant influence on any one or all of the key outputs of a process.

CTQ – See Critical to Quality.

Current Reality Tree – A problem-analysis tool used to examine cause and effect or logic behind current situation.

Cycle Time (ct) – The total amount of elapsed time expended from the time a task, product or service is started until it is completed.

# D

Defect – An output of a process that does not meet a defined specification, requirement or desire such as time, length, colour, finish, quantity, temperature etc.

Defective – A unit of product or service that contains at least one defect.

Demand Forecasting – Prediction of the levels of weekly or monthly product activity over a specified time (generally about two years).

Deployment (Six Sigma) – The planning, launch, training and implementation management of a Lean Six Sigma initiative within a company.

Design of Experiments – Generally, it is the discipline of using an efficient, structured and proven approach to interrogating a process or system for the purpose of maximising the gain in process or system knowledge.

DMAIC – The acronym for the five core phases of the Lean Six Sigma methodology – Define, Measure, Analyse, Improve and Control.

DPMO – Defects per Million Opportunities. The total number of defects observed divided by the total number of opportunities, expressed in parts per million. Sometimes called Defects per Million (DPM).

DPU – The total number of defects detected in some number of units divided by the total number of those units.

# E

Error Proofing – Error Proofing is a structured approach to ensure a quality and error free manufacturing environment. Error proofing assures that defects will never be passed to the next operation.

## F

Failure Mode and Effects Analysis (FMEA) – A procedure used to identify, assess and mitigate risks associated with potential product, system or process Failure Modes.

First In First Out (F.I.F.O.) – A system for keeping track of the order in which information or materials are to be processed. The goal of FIFO is to prevent earlier orders from being delayed in favour of newer orders which would result in increased lead time and unhappy customers regarding the earlier orders.

Fishbone Diagram – See Cause and Effect Diagram.

5 S – A methodology for organising, cleaning, developing, and sustaining a productive work environment. Improved safety, ownership of workspace, improved productivity and improved maintenance are some of the benefits of 5S program.

Flexible Manufacturing System (FMS) – A manufacturing process/system designed so that production areas (such as work cells or lines) can be changed and rebalanced often to adjust labour and materials to better meet and match demand.

Flowchart – A graphic model of the flow of activities, material and/or information that occurs during a process.

Future Reality Diagram/Tree – A sufficiency based logic structure designed to reveal how changes to the status quo would affect reality – specifically to produce desired effects.

## G

Gage R&R – Quantitative assessment of how much variation (repeatability and reproducibility) is in a measurement system compared to the total variation of the process or system.

Gemba – A Japanese term that means "Real Place" or "Where the action takes place." In Lean we speak of GEMBA as being the place where "Value" is added to a product. See Value Adding.

# H

Hidden Factory or Operation – Corrective and non-value-added work required to produce a unit of output that is generally not recognised as an unnecessary generator of waste in form of resources, materials and cost.

Histogram – A bar chart that depicts the frequencies (by the height of the plotted bars) of numerical or measurement categories.

# I

Ideal State Map – A future-looking version of a process map VSM (Value Stream Mapping) depicting how a process will work after improvements are implemented.

Input – A resource consumed, utilised or added to a process or system. Synonymous with X, characteristic, and input variable.

Input-Process-Output (IPO) Diagram – A visual representation of a process or system where inputs are represented by input arrows to a box (representing the process or system) and outputs are shown using arrows emanating out of the box.

Internal Customers – In a manufacturing environment "Internal Customers" are the people, machines, or processes being supplied with the products or parts made in preceding work area(s).

Internal Setup – Taken from SMED (Single-Minute Exchange of Die). These are setup procedures that can only be effected when a machine is in a "Zero Mechanical State".

Inventory Turnover Rate – The number of times an inventory cycles or turns over during the year. A frequently used method to compute inventory turnover is to divide average inventory level into annual cost of sales.

## J

JIT – A philosophy of manufacturing based on planned elimination of all waste and continuous improvement of productivity. It encompasses the successful execution of all manufacturing activities required to produce a final product.

## K

KanBan – A Japanese term meaning "visual record" or "card". In Lean Manufacturing speak, KanBan has come to mean "signal".

Knowledge-Based System – Software that uses artificial intelligence methods/systems and an information base regarding a specialised activity to control systems or operations.

## L

Last In First Out (LIFO) – The opposite of FIFO (First In First Out). With LIFO earlier orders are delayed in favour of newer orders which results in increased lead-time and unhappy customers regarding the earlier orders.

Lead-Time – The time required from receipt of order until products are shipped to a customer.

Lean Enterprise – An organisation that is engaged in the endless pursuit of waste elimination in all of its activities.

Lean Manufacturing – A manufacturing/production system best characterised as relentlessly eliminating waste from all of its activities and operations. Lean strives to produce products.

Lean Performance Indicator (LPI) – A consistent method to measure Lean implementation effectiveness.

Least Squares – A method of curve-fitting that defines the best fit as the one that minimises the sum of the squared deviations of the data points from the fitted curve.

Level-Loading and Mixed-Level-Loading – A technique used to balance production throughput according to the needs of customers.

Long-Term Variation – The observed variation of an input or output characteristic which has had the opportunity to experience the majority of the variation effects that influence it.

Lower Control Limit (LCL) – Used with Control Charts: the limit above which the subgroup statistics must remain for the process to be in control. Typically, 3 Standard Deviations below the central tendency.

Lower Specification Limit – The lowest value of a characteristic which is acceptable.

## M

Manufacturability – The extent to which a product can be efficiently manufactured with maximum reliability.

Measurement – The act of obtaining knowledge about an event or characteristic through measured quantification or assignment to categories.

Measurement Accuracy – For a repeated measurement, it is a comparison of the average of the measurements compare to some known standard.

Measurement Precision – For a repeated measurement, it is the amount of variation that exists in the measured values.

Measurement Systems Analysis (MSA) – An assessment of the accuracy and precision of a method of obtaining measurements. See also Gage R&R.

Metric – A measure that is considered to be a key indicator of performance. It should be linked to goals or objectives and carefully monitored.

Muda – See Waste.

## N

Natural Tolerances of a Process – See Control Limits.

Nominal Group Technique – A structured method that a team can use to generate and rank a list of ideas or items.

Non-Value Added (NVA) – Any activity performed in producing a product or delivering a service that does not add value, where value is defined as changing the form, fit or function of the product or service and is something for which the customer is willing to pay.

## O

Opportunities – The number of characteristics, parameters or features of a product or service that can be classified as acceptable or unacceptable.

Out of Control – A process is said to be out of control if it exhibits variations larger than its Control Limits or shows a pattern of variation.

Output – A resource or item or characteristic that is the product of a process or system. See also Y, CTQ.

Overall Equipment Effectiveness – Measures the availability, performance efficiency, and quality rate of equipment.

# P

Painted Floor – Coloured lines or shapes painted or taped on a floor that provide Visual Cues/Information.

Pareto Chart – A Bar Chart for Attribute (or categorical) Data categories presented in descending order of frequency.

Pareto Principle – The general principle originally proposed by Vilfredo Pareto (1848–1923) that the majority of influence on an outcome is exerted by a minority of input factors.

Poka-Yoke – A translation of a Japanese term meaning to mistake-proof.

Prerequisite Tree – A logical structure designed to identify all obstacles and the responses needed to overcome them in realising an objective. It identifies minimum necessary conditions without which the objective cannot be met.

Probability – The likelihood of an event or circumstance occurring.

Process Certification – Establishing documented evidence that a process will consistently produce a required outcome or meet required specifications.

Process Characterisation – The act of thoroughly understanding a process, including the specific relationship(s) between its outputs and the inputs, and its performance and capability.

Process Flow Diagram    – See Flowchart.

Process Member – A person who performs activities within a process to deliver a process output, a product or a service to a customer.

Process Route Table – Shows what machines and equipment are needed for processing a component or assembly. These tables aid in creating ordinary lines and grouping work pieces into work cells.

# Q

Quality Audit – A systematic and usually independent examination of a company's commitment to quality practices to verify if quality related activities are implemented effectively and comply with the company's or industry's quality systems and/or quality standards.

Quality Function Deployment (QFD) – A systematic process used to integrate customer requirements into every aspect of the design and delivery of products and services.

# R

Random Input – A lateral thinking tool that is useful when one needs fresh ideas or new perspectives during problem solving.

Range – A measure of the variability in a data set. It is the difference between the largest and smallest values in a data set.

Rapid Prototyping – A process that avoids creating conventional tooling thereby limiting investment expense while new parts or products are tested for feasibility of manufacture.

Reframing Matrix – A technique that helps to look at problems from a number of different viewpoints. It subsequently helps to expand the range of creative solutions.

Regression Analysis – A statistical technique for determining the mathematical relation between a measured quantity and the variables it depends on. Includes Simple and Multiple Linear Regression.

Repeatability – The extent to which repeated measurements of a particular object with a particular instrument produce the same value. See also Gage R&R.

Reproducibility – The extent to which repeated measurements of a particular object with a particular individual produce the same value. See also Gage R&R.

Rework – Activity required to correct defects produced by a process.

Risk Priority Number – The aggregate score of a failure mode including its severity, frequency of occurrence and ability to be detected.

Rolled Throughput Yield – The probability of a unit going through all process steps or system characteristics with zero defects.

Run Chart – A basic graphical tool that charts a characteristic's performance over time.

## S

Scatter Plot – A chart in which one variable is plotted against another to determine the relationship, if any, between the two.

Screening Experiment    – A type of experiment to identify the subset of significant factors from among a large group of potential factors.

Short-Term Variation – The amount of variation observed in a characteristic which has not had the opportunity to experience all the sources of variation from the inputs acting on it.

Sigma Score (Z) – A commonly used measure of process capability that represents the number of short-term Standard Deviations between the Centre of a process and the closest specification limit. Sometimes referred to as Sigma Level, or simply Sigma.

Significant Y – An output of a process that exerts a significant influence on the success of the process or the customer.

Single Minute Exchange of Die (SMED) – SMED is the Lean tool used to very quickly change machines or processes over from producing a specific part number or product to producing a different part number or product or changing an attribute(s) of the current part number or product. SMED processes are highly choreographed and rehearsed to minimise machine downtime.

Six Sigma – A scientific/data-driven approach for achieving 6 standard deviations between the mean and nearest specifications limit. Six Sigma methods can be applied to all aspects of manufacturing, transactional processes, and virtually any form of work or processing.

Special Cause Variation – Those non-random causes of variation that can be detected by the use of Control Charts and good process documentation.

Specification Limits – The bounds of acceptable performance for a characteristic.

Stability (of a process) – A process is said to be stable if it shows no recognisable pattern of change and no Special Causes of variation are present.

Standard Deviation – One of the most common measures of variability in a data set or in a population. It is the square root of the variance.

Standard Rate or Work – The length of time that should be required to set up a given machine or operation and run one part, assembly, batch, or end product through that operation. This time is used in determining machine requirements and labour requirements.

Standardised Work – Repeating work activities using the same processes every time.

Statistical Process Control (SPC) – The use of basic graphical and statistical methods for measuring, analysing and controlling the variation of a process for the purpose of continuously improving the process. A process is said to be in a state of statistical control when it exhibits only random variation.

Statistical Quality Control (SQC) – A procedure that applies the laws of probability and statistical processes to observed characteristics of a product or process.

Statistical Solution – A data driven solution with known confidence/risk levels, as opposed to a qualitative, "I think" solution.

Supply Chain Management – The tool used to pass data and expectations between suppliers and customers with the primary purpose being for the customers to have what is needed, in the quantity and quality needed, and at the lowest possible price.

Systems Integration – A process whereby all elements of a product are incorporated and usually tested in order to insure proper functions per customer specifications.

## T

Takt Time – The time required between completion of successive units of end product. Takt Time is used to pace lines in the production environments.

Theory of Constraints – A management philosophy that can be viewed as three separate but interrelated areas – logistics, performance measurement, and logical thinking. TOC focuses the organisation's scarce resources on improving the performance of the true constraint, and therefore the bottom line of the organisation.

Time to Market – The length of time it takes to develop a new product from inception until its first market sales.

Total Productive Maintenance (TPM) – A maintenance program concept, which brings maintenance into focus in order to minimise downtimes and maximise equipment usage. The goal of TPM is to avoid emergency repairs and keep unscheduled maintenance to a minimum.

Total Quality Management (TQM) – A Quality Control System focused on the correction of quality issues before they are permitted to subsequently be passed on for further processing. TQM systems are often "built-in" to manufacturing processes.

Transition Tree – A cause and effect logic tree designed to provide step-by-step progress from initiation to completion of a course of action or change.

True Capacity – The "real attainable volume" at full utilisation of a manufacturing system or subsystems after deducting for "normal events" such as machine maintenance, known bottlenecks, etc.

Two-Level Design – An experiment where all factors are set at one of two levels, denoted as low and high (-1 and 1).

## U

Upper Control Limit (UCL) for Control Charts – The Upper Limit below which a process statistic must remain to be in Control. Typically this value is 3 Standard Deviations above the central tendency.

Upper Specification Limit (USL) – The highest value of a characteristic which is acceptable.

## V

Value-Added (VA) – Any activity that makes a product more like what a customer is willing to pay for.

Value Added to Non-Value Added Lead Time Ratio – Provides insight on how many Value Added activities are performed compared to Non-Value Added activities, using time as a unit of measure.

Value Stream Mapping – Value Stream Mapping is a graphical tool that helps you to see and understand the flow of the material and information as a product makes its way through the value stream. It ties together Lean concepts and techniques.

Variability – A generic term that refers to the property of a characteristic, process or system to take on different values when it is repeated.

Variables – Quantities which are subject to change or variability.

Variance – A specifically defined mathematical measure of variability in a data set or population. It is the square of the Standard Deviation.

Variation – See Variability.

Virtual Prototyping – Software-based engineering process that includes the use of modelling in multiple dimensions and in software simulated "normal operating conditions" in order to discover weaknesses, design improvement opportunities, and general refinement before physically building a tangible prototype.

VOB – Voice of the Business. Represents the needs of the business and the key stakeholders of the business. It is usually items such as profitability, revenue, growth, market share, etc.

VOC – Voice of the Customer. Represents the expressed and non-expressed needs, wants and desires of the recipient of a process output, a product or a service. It is usually expressed as specifications, requirements or expectations.

VOP – Voice of the Process. Represents the performance and capability of a process to achieve both business and customer needs. It is usually expressed in some form of an efficiency and/or effectiveness metric.

## W

Waste – Any activity which utilises equipment, materials, parts, space, employee time or other corporate resource beyond the minimum amount required for value-added operations to insure manufacturability.

Work Cells – Generally a horseshoe or U-Shaped work area layout that enables workers to easily move from one process to another in close proximity and pass parts between workers with little effort. "Cells" typically focus on the production of specific models in "part families" but can be adjusted to many different products as needed.

Workflow Diagram – Shows the movement of material, identifying areas of waste. Aids teams to plan future improvements, such as one piece flow and work cells.

## X

X – An input characteristic to a process or system. In Lean Six Sigma it is usually used in the expression of $Y=f(X)$, where the output (Y) is a function of the inputs (X).

## Y

Y – An output characteristic of a process or system. In Lean Six Sigma it is usually used in the expression of $Y=f(X)$, where the output (Y) is a function of the inputs (X).

## Z

Z – Score. See Sigma Score.

# References

Adams, C.W., Gupta, P. &.Wilson, C.E. 2003. *Six Sigma deployment*. Boston: Butterworth-Heinemann.

Bertels, T., Rath & Strong. 2003. *Rath & Strong's Six Sigma leadership handbook*. NY: John Wiley & Sons.

Breyfogle, F. 2008. *Integrated enterprise excellence, Volume III improvement project execution: a management and black belt guide for going beyond Lean Six Sigma and the balanced scorecard*. Austin, TX: Citius Publishing, Inc.

Breyfogle, F. W. 1999. *Implementing Six Sigma: smarter solutions using statistical methods*. New York, NY: John Wiley & Sons.

Breyfogle, F.W., Cupello, J. M., & Meadows, B. 2001. *Managing Six Sigma*. New York: John Wiley and Sons.

Brue, G. & Howes, R. 2006. *The McGraw-Hill 36-hour course: Six Sigma*. NY: McGraw-Hill.

De Feo, J. A. & Barnard, W. 2005. *JURAN Institute's Six Sigma breakthrough and beyond: quality performance breakthrough methods*. Tata McGraw-Hill Publishing Company Limited

De Koning, H. & De Mast, J. 2007. The CTQ flowdown as a conceptual model of project objectives. *Quality Management Journal* 14, no. 2: 19-28.

De Mast, J. 2006. Six Sigma and competitive advantage. *Total Quality Management and Business Excellence* 17, no. 4: 455-465.

De Mast, J., Does, R. J. M. M. & De Koning, H. 2006. *Lean Six Sigma for service and healthcare*. Alphen aan den Rijn, the Netherlands: *Beaumont Quality Publications*

Fadem, T. J. 2009. *The art of asking: ask better questions, get better answers*. Upper Saddle River, NJ: Pearson Education, Inc.

George, M. 2003. Lean *Six Sigma for service: how to use lean speed and Six Sigma quality to improve services and transactions.* NY: McGraw-Hill.

Goleman, D., 1998. What makes a leader? *Harvard Business Review,* Vol.76, No.6.

Gupta, P. 2005. *The Six Sigma performance handbook: a statistical guide to optimizing results. Six Sigma operational methods series.* NY: McGraw-Hill Professional.

Gygi, C., DeCarlo, N., & Williams, B. 2005. *Six Sigma for dummies.* Hoboken, NJ: Wiley Publishing, Inc.

Hammett, E.H. & Pierce, J.R.; with DeVane S. 2009. *Making shifts without making waves: a coach approach to soulful leadership.* Chalice Press.

Harry, M. & Schroeder, R. 2000. *Six Sigma.* Random House, Inc.

Harry, M. J. 1988. *The nature of Six Sigma quality. Rolling Meadows,* Illinois: Motorola University Press.

Hersey, P. & Blanchard, K. 1993. *Management of organizational behavior: Utilizing human resources.* Englewood, NJ: Prentice Hall Inc.

Hoerl, R.W. & Snee, R.D. 2002. *Statistical thinking: improving business performance.* Pacific Grove, CA: Duxbury Press.

Keller, S. & Aiken, C. 2009. 'The inconvenient truth about change management: Why it isn't working and what to do about it.', The McKinsey Quarterly, April.

Kotter, J.P. 1995. *Sense of urgency.* Harvard Business Press.

Kotter, J.P. 2008. *Sense of urgency.* Harvard Business Press.

Montgomery, D. C. 2009. *Statistical quality control: a modern introduction,* 6th ed. Hoboken, New Jersey: John Wiley & Sons.

Miller, D. 2011. *Successful change: how to implement change through people.* Hayward's Heath, UK: Changefirst Ltd.

Oriel Incorporated. 2007. *Guiding successful Lean Six Sigma projects.* Madison, VA: Oriel Incorporated.

Pande, P.S., Neuman R.P. and Cavanagh, R.R. 2001. *The Six Sigma way team fieldbook: An implementation guide for process improvement teams.* NY: McGraw-Hill.

Rath & Strong Management Consultants, *Six Sigma Pocket Guide.*

Rock, D. 2006. *Quiet Leadership,* NY: Harper Collins.

Rock, D. 2009. *Your Brain at Work,* NY: Harper Collins.

Rock, D. 2007. *Intensive Coach Training,* Neuro Leadership Group.

Rosen, K. 2008. *Coaching salespeople into sales sponsors: A tactical playbook for managers and executives.* John Wiley & Sons.

Snee, R. D. & Hoerl, R.W. 2002. *Leading Six Sigma: a step-by-step guide based on experience with GE and other Six Sigma companies.* Upper Saddle River, NJ: FT Press.

Snee, R.D. & Hoerl, R.W. 2005. *Six Sigma beyond the factory floor: deployment strategies for financial services, health care, and the rest of the real economy.* Saddle River, NJ: FT Press.

Stamatis, D. H. 2004. *Six Sigma fundamentals: a complete guide to the system, methods, and tools.* New York, New York: Productivity Press.

Stoltzfus, T. 2008. *Coaching questions: a coach's guide to powerful asking skills.* Pegasus Creative Arts.

Tozer, J. 1997. *Leading initiatives: leadership, teamwork and the bottom line.* Port Melbourne: Butterworth-Heinemann.

Truscott, W. 2003. *Six Sigma: Continual improvement for businesses.* Butterworth-Heinemann.

# About the author

Morgan Jones has spent the last 25 years helping organisations implement change. He has extensive expertise in directly managing Lean Six Sigma deployment in Europe and Asia in various companies and industries, including banking, manufacturing, mining and service industries. He has trained over 250 Black Belts and 500 Green Belts in Lean Six Sigma, coaching them to deliver in excess of $370 million to the bottom line of their companies.

He frequently presents at international business improvement conferences in Australia and Asia, has chaired over 12 of them and regularly and is regularly head judge of process improvement awards.

Through 25 years of experience of change implementation, Morgan has developed a deep belief that to successfully sponsor projects, managers must build their own capability to transform themselves and not be dependent on external support.

His academic background is in engineering and management with a Masters in Manufacturing, Management and Doctorate in Competitive Strategy and he is an internationally registered Executive and Personal Coach. He has lived and worked in Europe and Asia as well as spending time working in the United States.

www.ingramcontent.com/pod-product-compliance
Lightning Source LLC
Chambersburg PA
CBHW061318220326
41599CB00026B/4933